SOME ASPECTS OF HITTITE RELIGION

View of Yazilikaya

SOME ASPECTS OF HITTITE RELIGION

O. R. GURNEY, F.B.A.

THE SCHWEICH LECTURES
OF THE BRITISH ACADEMY
1976

PUBLISHED FOR THE BRITISH ACADEMY
BY OXFORD UNIVERSITY PRESS
1977

Oxford University Press, Walton Street, Oxford OX2 6DP

OXFORD LONDON GLASGOW
NEW YORK TORONTO MELBOURNE WELLINGTON
IBADAN NAIROBI DAR ES SALAAM LUSAKA CAPE TOWN
KUALA LUMPUR SINGAPORE JAKARTA HONG KONG TOKYO
DELHI BOMBAY CALCUTTA MADRAS KARACHI

ISBN 0 19 725974 X

Printed in Great Britain
at the University Press, Oxford
by Vivian Ridler
Printer to the University

CONTENTS

LIST OF PLATES

ABBREVIATIONS

ABoT	*Ankara Arkeoloji Müzesinde bulunan Boğazköy Tabletleri* (*Boğazköy-Tafeln im Archäologischen Museum zu Ankara*). Istanbul, 1948.
AfO	*Archiv für Orientforschung.*
ANET	*Ancient Near Eastern Texts*, ed. J. B. Pritchard, 3rd edn., Princeton, 1969.
BiOr	*Bibliotheca Orientalis.*
CAD	*The Assyrian Dictionary* of the Oriental Institute of the University of Chicago.
CTH	E. Laroche, *Catalogue des textes hittites*. Paris, 1971.
HWb	J. Friedrich, *Hethitisches Wörterbuch*. Heidelberg, 1952.
IBoT	*Istanbul Arkeoloji Müzelerinde bulunan Boğazköy Tabletleri* (*Boğazköy-Tafeln im Archäologischen Museum zu Istanbul*): I, 1944; II, 1947; III, 1954.
JAOS	*Journal of the American Oriental Society.*
JBL	*Journal of Biblical Literature.*
JCS	*Journal of Cuneiform Studies.*
JKF	*Jahrbuch für Kleinasiatische Forschung.*
JNES	*Journal of Near Eastern Studies.*
KBo	*Keilschrifttexte aus Boghazköi*. Leipzig/Berlin, 1916– .
KUB	*Keilschrifturkunden aus Boghazköi*. Berlin, 1921– .
MDOG	*Mitteilungen der Deutschen Orient-Gesellschaft.*
MIO	*Mitteilungen des Instituts für Orientforschung.*
MVAG	*Mitteilungen der Vorderasiatisch-Aegyptischen Gesellschaft.*
OLZ	*Orientalistische Literaturzeitung.*
RHA	*Revue Hittite et Asianique.*
RHR	*Revue de l'Histoire des Religions.*
RlA	*Reallexikon der Assyriologie*. Berlin, 1928– .
SMEA	*Studi Micenei ed Egeo-anatolici.*
SPAW	*Sitzungsberichte der Preussischen Akademie der Wissenschaften.*
StBoT	*Studien zu den Boğazköy-Texten*. Wiesbaden, 1965– .
VBoT	A. Goetze, *Verstreute Boghazköi-Texte*. Marburg, 1930.
WVDOG	*Wissenschaftliche Veröffentlichungen der Deutschen Orient-Gesellschaft.*
ZA	*Zeitschrift für Assyriologie.*
ZAW	*Zeitschrift für die alttestamentliche Wissenschaft.*
ZDMG	*Zeitschrift der Deutschen Morgenländischen Gesellschaft.*

INTRODUCTION

In choosing subjects for these lectures I have had in mind the wishes of the founder, that they should have some reference to biblical studies. Historically the kingdom of Hattusa had little direct impact on the Hebrews of the Old Testament, since the Hittite Empire never extended south of Damascus. The possible connection between the Hittite treaties and the form of the Hebrew Covenant suggested itself, but this subject has been fully investigated, with a largely negative result.[1] The institutions of the Hittites, being partly of Indo-European, partly of Anatolian origin, again differ widely from those of the Hebrews. Such connections as have been established between the Hittites and the Hebrews belong in fact largely to the field of religion.[2]

Hittite religion in general has been well treated by several eminent authorities.[3] It has two distinct aspects: the local cults, each with its own traditions, and the State religion of the king, based on the capital, Hattusa. The local cults must go back into prehistoric times, with little change over the centuries. They fit easily into the pattern established by Robertson Smith for such popular cults nearly a century ago. The deity was the protector of the community, granting well-being and prosperity in return for daily service and attention. At the national level the king took over these services as supreme High Priest of the realm, and the texts of the royal library reveal how conscientiously the kings of the later Empire discharged their duties on behalf of the nation. They also reveal, in a series of remarkable prayers, a significant advance in theology.[4] In primitive religion the god was the god of the community. Should a member of the community commit an offence which aroused the god's anger, his whole family, even the whole community and future generations, could expect to suffer for it, with the result that punishment might fall on individuals who were themselves guiltless. But the Hittites saw their relationship to their god as that of a servant

[1] Mendenhall, 1954; Baltzer, 1960; especially McCarthy, 1963.

[2] They have been assembled by Hoffner, 1973, summarizing his earlier articles of 1967a, 1968 a–b, and 1969.

[3] Goetze, 1933a; Furlani, 1936; Dussaud, 1945; Laroche, 1946/7 (on the pantheon); Güterbock, 1949 and 1964; Otten, 1961a and 1964a; Kümmel, 1973a.

[4] Furlani, 1934, 1935, 1936; Houwink ten Cate, 1967, 1969. Furlani's penetrating analysis of the prayers in 1934 has been unjustly neglected.

to his master or as that of a subject to his king.[1] This was a relationship of individuals, and for the kings in their judicial capacity it was axiomatic that to punish a citizen for a crime he had not committed was a gross injustice. It was also usual for a master or for the king, when sitting in judgement, to treat an offender more leniently if he confessed his fault. The royal prayers are properly pleas of confession and self-defence (Hittite *arkuwar*) before the tribunal of the god;[2] but conflicting with this concept of the god as a just and humane judge there still survives the older religious view of a 'jealous god visiting the sins of the fathers upon the children'.[3] In the prayers of Mursili II on the occasion of the pestilence which was ravaging the country, a constant theme is that punishment is being inflicted for offences that were committed in a previous generation, that the culprits themselves are dead and gone and it is unjust to penalize the living.[4] But in a remarkable passage in his last prayer the king humbly confesses that he shares his father's guilt:[5]

> O Weather-god of Hatti, my lord, O gods, my lords, it is true, man is sinful. My father sinned and transgressed against the word of the Weather-god of Hatti, my lord. I have not sinned in any respect. It is true, however, that the father's sin falls upon the son. So my father's sin has fallen upon me. Now I have confessed before the Weather-god of Hatti and before the gods, my lords, (saying): 'It is true, we have done it.' And because I have confessed my father's sin, let the soul of the Weather-god of Hatti, my lord, and those of the gods, my lords, be appeased.

These matters, however, are not new. The prayers have been translated many times and have long since been exploited for the important contribution they have made to the history of religion. I have attempted in these lectures to select aspects of Hittite religion in which there have been recent and less well-known developments. In the second and third lectures I have discussed, among other things, two matters where a connection with the Old Testament seems well established: the *maṣṣēbâ* as a cult object, and the scapegoat ritual, together with other rites related to them. But one can hardly speak about a religion without giving some account of its gods, and in the first lecture I have tried to describe the pantheon of the Hittites, not, as has

[1] Furlani, 1935, 1938, based principally on the text 'Instructions for Temple Officials', *CTH* 264 (*ANET* 207–10).

[2] Laroche, 1964/5, 13–20. Houwink ten Cate, 1967, 101; 1969, 82 ff.

[3] Exod. 20: 5.

[4] Goetze, 1930; *CTH* 378 (*ANET* 394 ff.). Also Gurney, 1940 (*CTH* 376–7).

[5] On the development of Mursili's thought in successive prayers see Güterbock, 1960b, 61–2; Houwink ten Cate, 1969, 97–8.

usually been done, in its fully developed form as seen in texts of the later Empire, but diachronically in its historical development.

I should like here to express my thanks and appreciation to the British Academy for the honour they have conferred on me in inviting me to deliver these lectures. I only regret that I have not succeeded in finding a more closely integrated theme.

I

THE PANTHEON

EVERY writer on Hittite religion has remarked that the Hittite texts contain an enormous number of divine names, many of which are still no more than names to us. In speaking of the pantheon we are thinking primarily of the State religion, the gods and goddesses recognized and venerated in the capital and served by the official priesthood. This pantheon developed from simple beginnings into a highly complex system through an increasing tendency to gather in the local cults. Its most typical expression is seen in the later treaty lists, the lists of deities regularly invoked as witnesses when treaties were sworn with vassal kings and foreign powers and often summarized as 'the thousand gods of Hatti'.[1] It was these lists that formed the basis of Goetze's outline of the Hittite pantheon in his *Kulturgeschichte* of 1933,[2] and we may therefore take them as a starting point.

The order of the deities is fixed and only variable in minor details, from the treaty made by Suppiluliuma I with Hukkana of Hayasa down to the end of the Empire. At the head stood a male and a female Sun deity: the Sun-god of Heaven, King of the Lands, shepherd of mankind, and the Sun-goddess of Arinna, Queen of the Lands. Then comes a long list of Weather-gods, designated either by epithets or by cult-centres, among which Hattusa itself, Nerik, Zippalanda, Halap (Aleppo), and Arinna take a leading place. In some treaties the Weather-god's attendants, the bulls Seri and Hurri, the mountains Namni and Hazzi, are included here.[3] The next type is denoted by the logogram KAL, about which we shall have more to say. The gods Zithariya, Karzi, and Hapantaliya are attached to this group.

At this point the lists usually insert the Babylonian names Allatum (the Queen of the Underworld), Ea (the god of the sweet waters), and his wife Damkina;[4] one treaty also adds the name of Marduk.[5]

[1] Weidner, 1923; Friedrich, 1926/1930; Kühne–Otten, 1971.

[2] Goetze, 1933a, 122–3; 1957, 130–1.

[3] Only in Šattiwaza (Weidner, nos. 1–2) and Alaksandus (Friedrich, no. 5). On these deities see Haas and Röllig, 1975; on the name Šattiwaza, Zaccagnini, 1974.

[4] Damkina only in Šattiwaza (Weidner, nos. 1–2), following Ea. Allatum always precedes Ea (except in Tette, Weidner, no. 3) and is not a variant for Damkina, as seems to be implied

[*Note 4 continued and note 5 opposite*

The god Telipinu follows, with his cult-centres Tawiniya, Turmitta, and Hanhana, then in many treaties the pair Pirwa and Askasepa, followed by the goddess Ishtar, with her attendants Ninatta and Kulitta; the Moon-god and the goddess Ishhara, both special protectors of the oath, and the God of War in the guise of the logogram ZABABA, with whom are grouped Yarri, Zappana, and once Hasameli.[1]

Next come a group of local deities, each belonging to a particular cult-centre: Hantidassu (a title, 'the most powerful'[2]), Apara, Kattahha, 'the Queen',[3] Ammamma, Hallara, Huwassana,[4] *BELAT* 'the lady',[5] and Kunniyawanni. The gods of the foreign mercenaries, Lulahhi and Hapiri, are added here.

There follows a group of deities of the Nether World. At their head stands their queen, designated sometimes by the Sumerian name Erishkigal, sometimes as 'Sun-goddess of the Earth', i.e. the Underworld—this regardless of the fact that Allatum, who occurs earlier in the list, is essentially the same goddess.[6] And after her come a constantly recurring group called 'the Primeval Gods', namely Nara, Napsara, Minki, Ammunki, Tuhusi, Ammizadu, with whom are closely associated the Sumerian deities Alalu, Anu, Antu, Enlil, and Ninlil, and (in one treaty only) Bēlat-ekalli.[7]

The list ends with the mountains, rivers, springs, the Great Sea, heaven and earth, winds and clouds. All are nameless except in two treaties, one of which names two mountains, Hulla

by Goetze (1957, 130); the name is here an Akkadogram for the Hattian Lelwani, as shown by Otten, 1950, 119. On this deity see below, pp. 12, 16.

5 Hukkanas (Friedrich, no. 6); probably representing Sanda (see below, pp. 29–30).

1 Only in Šattiwaza.

2 Laroche, 1946/7, 73.

3 Although *kattaḫ* is Hattic for 'queen', Kattahha and 'the Queen'—the latter usually written logographically—are goddesses of different cities, Ankuwa and Katapa respectively. In later texts the name Kattahha developed into Hatagga, the meaning having evidently been lost (Kühne and Otten, 1971, 49 f.). According to Goetze, 1953, 265, there was yet another goddess called 'Queen', namely Kattahzipuri, on whom see below, p. 13. The name of the goddess of Katapa appears once as ^{d}*Ḫa-*. . . .; Laroche, 1946/7, 104, suggests the reading Hassusara.

4 On this deity see Güterbock, 1962; Goetze, 1963, 93; Frantz-Szabó, 1975.

5 The goddess of Landa is always so written. The name concealed by the Akkadogram might be Hurrian Allani, which has the same meaning; but the other deity of Landa, Kunniyawanni, has a Luwian name. Cf. Burde, 1974, 13.

6 In some treaties Erishkigal is separated from the following group by the summary 'Male and female gods of . . .'; but she certainly belongs with them, as in the two treaties with Šattiwaza and in the treaty with Manapa-Tarhuntas (Friedrich, 1930, 16) where she is replaced by the 'Sun-goddess of the Underworld' (here = Hurrian Allani, see Laroche, 1974). In the earlier position this same title appears in the Hukkana treaty with *ALLATUM* representing the Hattian goddess Lelwani (see p. 4 n. 4, and p. 16).

7 The wife of Ninurta, assimilated into the Hurrian pantheon as Pentikalli (Goetze, 1940; Laroche, 1968, 529).

and Zaliyanu,[1] and the other (with Mitanni) the rivers Tigris and Euphrates.[2]

These lists are supplemented by the prayer of Muwatalli,[3] which enumerates the pantheon in order of cult centres. Additional items contributed by this text are as follows.

The pantheon of Arinna includes, beside the Sun-god, Sun-goddess, and Weather-god, the goddesses Mezulla and Zintuhi and Mount Hulla.

Hattusa itself has a pantheon, which includes, beside the Weather-god and the god KAL of Hatti, the goddess Hebat, the Babylonian pair Ea and Damkina, the deified throne Halmasuitta, Allatum, Ishtar of Nineveh, the Lulahhi gods, the goddess Kubaba, also Pirwa, Askasepa, Karzi, and Hapantalli.

The god Zithariya is located at a city Zithara.

Telipinu appears not only at Tawiniya, Turmitta, and Hanhana, but also with the goddess Zashapuna and with Mt. Zaliyanu as deities of Kastama, a place closely linked with the holy city Nerik.

The goddess designated by the logogram MAḪ is listed under a city Sahhaniya and a goddess Tasimi under Lihzina.

A number of lesser deities are also mentioned.

Both the treaty lists and the prayer present virtually the complete Hittite pantheon, but the treaty lists are manifestly a compilation made for this particular purpose. The Sun-god stands at the head of the list as god of justice. He is almost a replica of the Akkadian Shamash. However, the gods who help the king in battle, for example, do not include the Sun-god. Here we find countless times at the head of the list the Sun-goddess of Arinna and the Weather-god of Hatti. It is the Weather-god, not the Sun-god, who is represented as concluding the treaty with the Egyptian Sun-god on behalf of the Hittite State, and he was regarded as the husband of the Sun-goddess of Arinna. Thus even at the height of the Hittite Empire there was no single unitary hierarchy of gods. The priests in their service to the king evidently undertook to reduce the proliferation of local cults to a coherent system, but the system they constructed does not give a true picture. Many deities who had a significant place in Hittite religion and appear in the prayer are unaccountably omitted from the treaties, among them

[1] Alaksandus (Friedrich, no. 5). On these mountains see Gonnet, 1968, 123, 144.

[2] Šattiwaza (Weidner, nos. 1–2). Doubtless 'local colour'.

[3] *CTH* 381.

Mezulla, Halmasuit, the Mother-goddess MAḪ and the young god Sarruma. Now, though the systematized treaty-list varies little from the reign of Suppiluliuma to the end of the Empire, its beginnings can be seen in the fragmentary treaty of Arnuwanda I, a predecessor of Suppiluliuma, with the Kaska folk.[1] Here we find only the Sun-god of Heaven, the Weather-god, the gods KAL and ZABABA, the goddesses whose names appear in the guise of Ishtar and Ishhara, and the group of Primeval gods. Here all local deities are omitted, even the Sun-goddess of Arinna. They are simply the great types, with the addition of Ishhara and the Primeval Gods, but omitting Kubaba and Halmasuit, the deified throne. This short list is surely significant. The concept of the 'Thousand Gods of Hatti' had not yet developed. We may now attempt to trace the official pantheon back to its origins.

The Hittite population was the product of the mixture of an indigenous stock, speaking a mainly prefixing language which we call Hattic, with invading groups of Indo-Europeans. The advent of these Indo-Europeans lies before the threshold of history and it has so far proved impossible to identify their arrival with the appearance of any particular archaeological culture. However, a recently translated text may possibly throw a glimmer of light on that distant time. This is the Legend of Zalpa, which was first published by Emil Forrer in 1926 but was augmented in 1970 by the discovery of a new fragment.[2]

According to this tale, the queen of Kanesh gave birth to thirty sons. Apparently in dismay at this portent she placed them in a box of some sort (one is reminded of the legend of Sargon of Akkad) and consigned the box to the river, where it drifted down to the sea and arrived at Zalpa. There the gods found it and raised the boys to manhood. Meanwhile, the queen of Kanesh had given birth to thirty daughters and decided to bring them up herself. The sons, on growing to manhood, set out from Zalpa to search for their mother. On arrival at Tamarmara they learnt that the queen of Kanesh had once given birth to thirty sons who had disappeared. Joyfully they exclaimed: 'What seek we further? We have found our mother.' On their arrival at Kanesh the queen failed to recognize them and gave them her thirty daughters, but the youngest warned his brothers against the incest they were about to commit. The

[1] *CTH* 139. The palaeography shows that this text must be a forerunner, not a condensed version, of the standard lists (Neu, 1968; Otten, 1974, etc.). Cf. Laroche, 1974, 177.

[2] Now fully edited by Otten, 1973a.

text here breaks off, but the last words suggest that his warning went unheeded. Whether he himself refrained from the crime remains unknown. After a lacuna, we are back in Zalpa, where the Sun-god pronounces a blessing. The rest of the mutilated text consists of a long account of hostilities between Zalpa and Hattusa, with which we are not concerned. The text ends with the destruction of Zalpa.

In spite of the fairy-tale character of this story it could well contain a kernel of historical tradition. Kanesh, the centre of Assyrian commercial activity in the preceding centuries, appears at one time to have had a queen (*rubātum*),[1] though the place was captured by Anitta from a king. Other Old Hittite texts refer to Zalpa as being by the sea (there was another place of the same name on the Euphrates). The journey of the brothers from Zalpa on the Black Sea to Kanesh and their marriage to the daughters of the queen may well be a reminiscence of an immigration from the north, as suggested by the editor, H. Otten. They would not then, of course, have been the queen's sons, but Mrs. S. R. Bin-Nun has proposed to see in this feature of the legend a memory of an ancient Anatolian custom of brother–sister marriage, which the Hittites themselves later abolished and regarded with strong disapproval.[2] Hence the attitude of the youngest brother.

In this legendary text the only deity mentioned is the Sun, written ^{d}UTU-*uš*.[3]

Another early text is the fragmentary saga about the first passage through the Taurus.[4] Here the Sun deity, again in the form ^{d}UTU-*uš*, gives orders to the army, apparently substituting for the king himself. This form of the name would later certainly be taken as the name of the male Sun-god, Istanus; but Carruba has well suggested that here it is simply the early form of the late title ^{d}UTU-*ŠI* and actually denotes the king.[5] Another deity who appears in this saga, though in a broken context, is the goddess Inara of Hattusa. This deity is one of several who are later written with the logogram KAL and her appearance in this early legend is significant.[6] She is the local genius of

[1] Otten, 1973a, 14. [2] Bin-Nun, 1975, 146.

[3] Text B, obv. 4 (with the plain logogram in lines 3 and 5).

[4] *CTH* 16. Otten, 1963a; 1964b, 117 f. [5] Carruba, 1969, 232 n. 22.

[6] Otten, 1954/6. The same logogram ^{d}KAL is also used for a totally different deity, the god on the stag, called by some 'Tutelary God' (*Schutzgott*), the logogram being read ^{d}LAMA. The reading of this god's Hittite name is disputed. Proposed readings: Kurunda (Houwink ten Cate, 1961, 128 ff.; Gordon, 1967, 71 n. 4), Tuwata (Laroche, 1954, 107 ff.), Uruwanda (Goetze, 1954b, 80; Carruba, 1968); in post-Hittite inscriptions the name appears as Runda. Ruwada, Rutia, (Greek) Ρωνδ(α). See Laroche, 1966, 289 ff., 295; 1960b,

Hattusa, and when she is said elsewhere to have handed over her house to the king,[1] this could be an allusion to the first Hittite occupation of that city.

If these semi-mythical texts refer to events of the remote past, those described in the Proclamation of Anitta[2] are certainly later. Anitta, king of Nesa (Kanesh) and Kussara, is a historical character mentioned in contemporary documents. He captured Hattusa and declared the city accursed. In this factual document we meet not only the Sun and the Weather-god but also other deities of considerable interest: the Throne-goddess Halmasuit, and a god who is called simply Sius-summis, apparently 'Our God'. The Weather-god, written ᵈIŠKUR-*unnaš*, functions as supreme patron of Anitta and his father and guarantor of the curse on Hattusa. Anitta builds temples at Kanesh for him and for 'Our God', whose statue at Kanesh had been carried off as plunder to Zalpa but recovered by Anitta. It is clear that 'Our God' was in a special way the god of Kanesh. His function is to deliver Hattusa into Anitta's hands, but the text substitutes Halmasuit, the Throne-goddess, for the name of Anitta.[3] She is evidently the deified throne itself, symbolizing the royal office, as we might say 'the Crown'.

Who then is 'Our God'? The editor of the Anitta text, E. Neu, has devoted a long discussion to this question. The noun *šiuš* is well known in later Hittite as the general word for 'god', cognate with Indo-European **di̯ēus* 'heaven', Greek *Zeus*, Latin, *dies*, *deus*, from a root meaning 'to shine'. Dr. Neu and, simultaneously but independently, Mrs. S. R. Bin-Nun,[4] have drawn attention to the correspondence between this and another Old Hittite text, the ritual for the erection of a new palace,[5] in respect of the deities mentioned: in the one, Weather-god, Throne-goddess, and 'Our God', in the other Weather-god, Throne-goddess, and Sun-god. The passage in the ritual runs:

> To me, the king, have the gods—Sun-god and Weather-god—entrusted the land and my house. I, the king, will rule over the land and my house. . . . To me, the king, the Throne-goddess has brought from the sea the power and the chariot.

nos. 102, 103; for the iconography, von Brandenstein, 1943, 78 ff.; and for this god's role in mythology, Güterbock, 1961b, 161 ff. (*CTH* 343).

[1] *KBo*. III. 7. ii. 15–20 (*CTH* 321; Laroche, 1965/8, 68; Haas, 1970, 149).
[2] *CTH* 1; Neu, 1974.
[3] On this goddess see Kretschmer, 1950, 416 ff.; Laroche, 1946/7, 21 f.; Archi, 1966.
[4] Bin-Nun, 1975, 150.
[5] *CTH* 414; *ANET* 357 ff.; Schwartz, 1947.

In this intriguing text we seem again to have a recollection of the king having come from a place near the sea to acquire the kingdom of Hattusa, with the Throne-goddess acting as the agent for the two high gods. The Throne-goddess indeed plays a leading role in this text. She is addressed by the king as his 'friend', but she is asked to stay 'behind the mountains' and keep to her own domain. Since her name, Halmasuit, is purely Hattian, she can hardly represent the king's original kingdom 'by the sea'. Her prominence here must surely mean that the king had taken over a Hattian kingdom and a Hattian throne but wished to keep his new subjects at a distance. Her association in this text with the Sun-god and the Weather-god has led Dr. Neu and Mrs. Bin-Nun to the conclusion that 'Our God' of the Anitta text is in reality the Sun-god, to be translated 'Our god Siu', the name being another cognate of the Greek Zeus, the 'god of heavenly light'.[1] That Anitta calls him 'our Siu' must mean that he identified himself closely with the city Kanesh, which he had inherited from his father. The later male Sun-god Istanus would represent this ancient Indo-European god under a new name, adopted and adapted from the indigenous Hattian Sun-goddess Estan by the addition of a Hittite stem vowel and case ending. When this occurred, according to this theory, the old name Sius was generalized in Hittite as a word for 'god', though in Luwian and Palaic it remained, in the cognate forms Tiwaz and Tiyaz, as the name for the Sun-god.

It is perhaps paradoxical that Zeus, the Thunderer, Τερπικέραυνος, should appear in Hittite, not as the Weather-god (^{d}IŠKUR) but as a Sun-god (^{d}UTU). However, the suggestion earlier made by Macqueen that the writing ^{d}IŠKUR-*unna*- represents *šiuna*-[2] can no longer be sustained, since on the one hand Laroche has shown that the name of the Weather-god in Hittite was Tarhu-, with a form Tarhunna-,[3] and on the other, Neu has established the early form of the nominative as *šiuš*, with *šiunaš* as genitive only.[4] It is a fact that the base **diēus* (with suffix *-att-*) produced the name of the Sun-god in Luwian and Palaic. Perhaps then it is possible that the simple stem should have done so in Hittite.

If this thesis is accepted, we find the earliest Hittite kings venerating the old Indo-European sky-god, now regarded as a sun-god, under the name Sius, and a Weather-god who may be the indigenous Hattian Taru, but under the new name

[1] German *Himmelsgott* (*Lichtgott*).
[2] Macqueen, 1959, 180.
[3] Laroche, 1958a, 93–4. Cf. Gordon, 1967, 83.
[4] Neu, 1974, 122.

Tarhunna. If the Hattian sun-deity Estan was indeed a goddess,[1] it would be difficult otherwise to explain why the Hittite Istanus is a male god. The goddess took on the personality of an ancient Indo-European god.

Beside these two great gods the only reference in these earliest texts is to the Throne-goddess, Halmasuit, whose name is purely Hattian, and to the god Telipinu, another Hattian god, who appears in the palace ritual as a kind of minister bringing wine for the assembly of the gods.

Mrs. Bin-Nun has drawn attention to the apparently universal character of these two deities, the Sun-god and the Weather-god, in the early texts. They appear together also in the early lustration ritual for the royal pair,[2] in the Old Hittite thunder ritual,[3] and in the ritual against the machinations of Ziplantawiya.[4] In all these texts the name of the Weather-god must be Tarhunna or Tarhunta. The name of the Sun-god is written ^{d}UTU-*uš* wherever the nominative case-ending is indicated. This is usually taken as Istanus, but it is only in the latest of these texts, the ritual against Ziplantawiya, where the genitive is ^{d}UTU-*waš*, that the reading Sius would not be equally possible.

It is necessary to look rather closely at these divine names because in the six-year annals of Hattusili I we find, not the Sun-god ^{d}UTU-*uš*, but the Sun-goddess of Arinna, who here makes her earliest textual appearance. Hattusili declares himself 'beloved of the Sun-goddess of Arinna' and brings back booty to her temple, as well as to those of the Weather-god and Mezulla. This text exists only in late copies and it is claimed that the addition of ^{uru}*Arinna* is due to the late scribe, the original having referred like these other early documents to the male Sun-god.[5] However, I do not think that the reference can be disposed of so easily. The Sun-goddess twice has the epithet GAŠAN-*IA* 'my lady'. This, it is true, is only in the Hittite

[1] (Nom.) *eš-ta-a-an* (= Hitt. ^{d}UTU-*uš*, *CTH* 726. 1 obv. 3) and apparently ^{d}UTU-*un*; (gen.) ^{d}*Aš-ta-nu-*(*u-*)*un* and ^{d}UTU-*un*; full references *apud* Kammenhuber, 1962, 5–6 (add *KBo* XXI. 85. i. 12 for gen.). On the strength of the equation with Istanus Friedrich, 1952, 146, Kammenhuber (1962, 7), Otten (1964a, 99), and von Schuler (1965b, 198) assume that this deity is male. But a Hattian Sun-deity written *li-e-*^{d}UTU, *KUB* XXVIII. 75. ii. 21, with Hittite 'translation' ^{d}UTU-*uš*, 205/s ii. 12 (*apud* Neu, 1974, 126) has the epithet 'queen' (*kattaḫ*/SAL.LUGAL) and is clearly a goddess. Laroche (1947, 198 and 1958b, 45) would read this *leštan*, though without any clear explanation of the prefix, which should be possessive 'his' with a plural noun. The reading is emphatically rejected by Kammenhuber, who regards this as a different sun-deity (1962, 7; 1969, 434). But no other name for a Hattian sun-deity is known, and the Hittite translator made no distinction. Until *Eštan* is found with a clear male epithet we may perhaps adopt the explanation proposed by Neu and outlined above.

[2] *CTH* 416; Otten and Souček, 1969.

[3] *CTH* 631; Neu, 1970.

[4] *CTH* 443; Szabó, 1971.

[5] Neu, 1974, 127.

version; but both versions describe the Sun-goddess as leading the king into battle, just as in later texts, and both versions refer constantly to the temple of Mezulla, a goddess everywhere else so closely associated with her mother, the Sun-goddess of Arinna, that in passages where she is coupled with the undetermined ^{d}UTU, most authorities assume that this is an abbreviation for 'Sun-goddess of Arinna'.[1] Indeed, since one of these passages is in the Old Hittite thunder ritual, the annals of Hattusili I should probably be cited as the earliest evidence for the Sun-goddess in the Old Kingdom rather than for the Sun-god. She is undoubtedly a Hattian goddess, for whom the name Wurusemu is attested in later texts.[2] Her relationship to the Hattian sun-deity Estan, especially if she is also a goddess, is a problem remaining to be solved.

Of other Hattian deities, we have already mentioned Halmasuit, the Throne-goddess, Inara, the genius of Hattusa, and Telipinu.[3] Others occurring in the rituals of the Old Kingdom are the War-god, Wurunkatte (who appears in the treaty-lists under the logographic ZABABA),[4] Siwat the 'Lucky Day',[5] Tasimmet the Weather-god's concubine,[6] and in an Underworld context, Lelwani (at this period a god, not a goddess),[7] Istustaya and Papaya, the Parcae who spin the threads of fate,[8] Kait the grain goddess,[9] Hasammeli the smith(?),[10] and

[1] Neu, 1970, 44 n. 2; Kammenhuber, 1971, 146, 157.

[2] *KUB* XXVIII. 6 (*CTH* 731); I. 17 (*CTH* 591, 3); XXVIII. 64 (*CTH* 745); 104 (*CTH* 744); XXXVI.89 (*CTH* 671, Haas, 1970, 140 ff., with variant spellings, cf. Macqueen, 1959, 175 ff.). None of these texts is in 'old ductus' (Neu, 1974, 127); XXXVI. 89 dates from the reign of Hattusilis III (Haas, 1970, 141); I. 17 is apparently 'a product of the deliberate amalgamation of cults which began with Hattusilis III' (Kammenhuber, 1971, 158). None the less, this must surely be a very ancient, pre-Hittite, name for the goddess (cf. Kammenhuber, 1969, 433). The meaning of the name is no better understood today than it was thirty years ago: '*šemu* of the country' (Laroche, 1946/7, 38; Kammenhuber, 1969, 447).

[3] In Hattian texts Talipinu, which may be regarded as the original form of the name. Against the earlier view of this god as a god of vegetation and agriculture (Goetze, 1933, 134; Laroche, 1946/7, 34; von Schuler, 1965, 201 f.), Güterbock (1959) has emphasized his affinity with the Weather-gods and has been followed by Haas, 1970, 106–7, though Otten (1968, 15) regards these characteristics as secondary. He has been compared with the Mysian hero Telephos (Kretschmer, 1930, 13) and with Apollo Delphinios (Barnett, 1956, 219).

[4] The name means 'King of the country'.

[5] Usually written ^{d}UD.SIG$_5$, but with a number of logographic variants (Laroche, 1946/7, 106; Otten, 1950, 126 ff.; 1958a, 13, 135 ff.; Goetze, 1953, 267; Neu, 1970, 41). The Hittite reading is (*assus*) *siwaz*, though apparently *Izzistanu* is also an equivalent (Otten, 1958a, 77 n. 1; Kammenhuber, 1962, 8; 1969, 434; Steiner, 1966, 551b). The name is a euphemism for 'Day of death' (Steiner, loc. cit.) and is especially frequent in the mortuary rituals.

[6] Otten, 1950, 123 ff.; Güterbock, 1961a, 16 f.; Laroche, 1966, 252 f.; Haas, 1970, 88.

[7] Otten, 1950, 129; Kammenhuber, 1972, 299.

[8] Bossert, 1957; Güterbock, 1961b, 149; Vieyra, 1965, 130.

[9] Laroche, 1946/7, 26; Kammenhuber, 1969, 460 f.; von Weiher, 1975, 60 (s.v. Halki). Kait is a goddess, though the equivalent Hittite Halki is apparently male.

[10] Kammenhuber, 1969, 436, 478; 1972, 298; but cf. von Weiher, 1975, 127. The great smith is bidden to 'take copper hammer and iron nails' in *CTH* 726.1. If this indeed refers to

Zilipuri.[1] In the Hattian myth of 'The Moon that fell from Heaven' we meet Hapantalli the Sun-god's shepherd and the goddess Kattahzipuri, with Kasku the Moon-god.[2] Other Hattic names are Sulinkatte (identified with Nergal)[3] and Zithariya, a god apparently represented by a shield which was carried in procession.[4] The 'gods of Kanesh' must also have been recognized by the people at this time, since their names appear in the onomastic of the pre-Hittite Assyrian colonies.[5] They include Pirwa, an equestrian form of Ishtar,[6] Ilali,[7] Tarawa,[8] and Assiyat.[9] Later, however, these gods are addressed in Luwian,[10]

Such are the principal gods and goddesses of the Hittite Old Kingdom. But the six-year annals of Hattusili also give us, by contrast, a glimpse into an entirely different pantheon of North Syria at this time. After capturing Hassuwa (near the Euphrates), Hattusili deports to Hattusa among other booty the Weather-god of Aleppo, the goddess Allatum, the god Atalur, (a local mountain god), the goddess Lilluri, and the goddess Hebat 'daughter of Allatum'.[11] In the Alaḷakh tablets (from the same area) Hebat and the Weather-god of Aleppo are associated with a goddess Ishtar or Ishhara. These are the gods of the Hurrians. They were to play a major part in Hittite religion, but it is clear from the annals of Hattusili that they had not yet crossed the Taurus.

The Hurrian cultural invasion begins in the fifteenth century, at the time when a queen with the Hurrian name Nikalmati appears in the Hittite dynastic lists as the wife of Tudhaliya II.[12] The name of this queen and that of her successor, Asmunikal, contain the name of Ningal, the wife of the Babylonian Moon-god Sin, and one of the most characteristic effects of the

the god Hasammeli mentioned a few lines later (denied by von Weiher, loc. cit.), there could be a connection with this god's other function of concealment by darkness and tightening doors and shutters (Goetze, 1953, 269–70). Goetze compares the name Kadmilos, Kasmilos, one of the Kabeiroi.

[1] Laroche, 1946/7, 39.

[2] Kammenhuber, 1955; *ANET* 120. Kattahzipuri, here equated with Kamrusepa, is elsewhere the high goddess of the Palaites (Kammenhuber, 1962, 77 f.). For Hapantalli as shepherd see Haas and Wilhelm, 1974, 24 f. The sheep or cattle of the Sun-god reappear in Classical mythology; cf. Page, 1973, 79 f.

[3] Laroche, 1946/7, 31; 1955c, 112; Haas, 1970, 72 ff.

[4] Otten, 1959b, 355–8; Güterbock, 1964, 68.

[5] Goetze, 1954a; Laroche, 1966, 288.

[6] Otten, 1953b; Güterbock, 1961a, 14; von Schuler, 1965b, 190 f.

[7] Laroche, 1966, 288; Goetze, 1953, 277.

[8] Goetze, 1953, 271; Friedrich, 1957, 224; Carruba, 1966, 30.

[9] Goetze, 1953, 274; Laroche, 1966, 289.

[10] Laroche, 1959, 126 f.

[11] Otten, 1958c, 82; Goetze, 1962, 28.

[12] Kammenhuber, 1974, 158.

Hurrian westward penetration was the importation of Babylonian deities in Hurrian guise, in particular Ea, with his wife Damkina, Anu and Antu, Enlil and Ninlil, and the goddesses Ishhara and Bēlat-ekalli, all of whom we have already noted in the later treaty lists. The ancestral gods of the Hurrians appear to have been the Weather-god Teshub, the Sun-god Shimegi, the Moon-god Kusuh, the War-god Astabi, an elder deity named Kumarbi, who was equated with the Babylonian Enlil, and the goddess Sausga, who was identified with Ishtar. These are found wherever Hurrians settled.[1] It was in Syria, however, that the Hurrian pantheon was formed which exercised such an influence on the Hittites. The great goddess Hebat (thought by some to have been the origin of the biblical Eve, or of the Classical Hekate)[2] belongs to this area, together with her mother Allatum or Allani[3] and Kubaba, the goddess of Carchemish.[4] Nikkal (Ningal) was probably borrowed from Harran. The Hurrian Kumarbi was equated with Dagan, the god of the middle Euphrates, and took over his wife Šalaš or Šaluš.[5] Kumarbi himself, to judge from his name, may have originated in Babylonia as the god of the Sumerian town Kumara,[6] but if so, his origin had long since been forgotten.

The accession of Tudhaliya II and Nikalmati marks the beginning of the period called either Middle Hittite or 'Archäisch Junghethitisch'. We have already noted a treaty of Arnuwanda from this period with an embryonic list of divine witnesses. We may now look at this list again in a new light.

The Sun-god of Heaven, explicitly so called, has not appeared before except as the physical orb in the sky towards which smoke ascends in the annals of Hattusili, and once in a broken line of the ritual of the royal pair. Presumably this is the god Istanus. The Sun-goddess of Arinna is conspicuous by her absence. The Weather-god is unspecified. The deity KAL could be either the goddess Inara, one of the ancient Hattian pantheon, or the stag-god Kurunda(?), another ancient Anatolian deity.[7] The logogram ZABABA stands for the Hattian

[1] Laroche, 1968, 522–7. On Sausga cf. Bossert, 1955, 74 ff., Danmanville, 1962.

[2] Hebat = Eve, Hrozný, 1932, 121; = Hekate, Barnett, 1956, 220. For this goddess in general see now Danmanville, 1975.

[3] Laroche, 1961, 84; 1968, 525; 1969, 93; 1974, 184 f. Allani is the Hurrian Queen of the Underworld.

[4] Laroche, 1960a.

[5] Laroche, 1968, 522–4.

[6] Cf. Forrer, 1936, 702 ff. Astour, 1968, on the other hand, would derive the name from a small town in Syria mentioned in Egyptian sources.

[7] See above, p. 8 n. 6. For the problem of a Hurrian counterpart see Güterbock *apud* Bittel, 1975, 174 f.

god Wurunkatte. But what of the two goddesses, Ishhara and Ishtar? Ishhara belongs to the Hurrian pantheon, imported from Babylon, and the writing 'Ishtar', with stem-vowel *-i-*, presumably refers, as it does elsewhere, to the goddess of Nineveh. Here, it seems, are the first signs of the Hurrian cultural invasion. The two Hurrian goddesses are grafted on to an ancient Hattian pantheon.

Moreover, in this early treaty we already find at the end of the list the strange group of 'Primeval Gods', Nar(r)a, Napsara, Minki, Ammunki, Tuhusi, and Ammizadu, though the Mesopotamian deities Alalu, Anu, Antu, Enlil, and Ninlil, who follow them in the later treaties, are here missing. These Primeval Gods were equated by the Hittites with the Anunnaki, the great gods of the Sumerians, an earlier generation of gods who had been banished to the Underworld by Teshub and had their home there.[1] The myth 'Kingship in Heaven' tells of this theomachy, and though the gods so banished in the myth are Alalu, Anu, and Kumarbi, the close connection with the other 'Primeval Gods' is shown by the fact that they are directly addressed in the proem to the tale.[2] They appear indeed to be a group of originally Mesopotamian deities whose names have been garbled in the process of transmission. Minki and Ammunki seem somehow to reflect either the primordial pair Enki and Ninki, or else Enki-Ea and either his epithet Ammanki or his dialect form Umunki. Narru was a name of Enlil. Is Napsara a corruption of Namtar, the dread messenger of the Underworld? Ammizadu may or may not be the Babylonian king Ammizaduga of Venus Tablet fame,[3] but it is difficult to see why this rather undistinguished Babylonian king should appear in such company. In any case the 'Primeval Gods' regularly occur in a Hurrian milieu and this would be in keeping with their Mesopotamian origin.[4]

The great enlargement of the Hittite pantheon which resulted in the stereotyped treaty lists of the Empire seems to have occurred shortly after 1400 B.C. This influence came immediately from Kizzuwadna, but more generally from Syria, which was

[1] Otten, 1961b, 115; Reiner and Güterbock, 1967, 265 f.

[2] Güterbock, 1946, 6 ff.; Goetze, *ANET* 120 f.; Güterbock, 1961b, 155 ff.; Laroche, 1965/8, 153.

[3] So Laroche, 1946/7, 127. A derivation from a place-name in Syria is suggested by Astour (1968, 173).

[4] For the 'Primeval Gods' in general see Forrer, 1936, 697 ff.; Gurney, 1940, 81; Laroche, 1946/7, 126; Güterbock, 1964, 55; Goetze, 1963, 96; Steiner, 1971, 273 ff.; Haas and Wilhelm, 1974, 51 ff.; Laroche, 1974, *passim*. Their queen, written Erishkigal (see above, p. 5 n. 6), must be understood as Allani in view of their Hurrian origin.

the scene of most of Suppiluliuma's conquests at this time. Kizzuwadna, with its capital Kummanni, the later Comana Cappadociae, was a country of mixed Luwian and Hurrian culture, and it is from there that the Hittites imported a great mass of rituals, mainly magical, and typically performed by the so-called 'Old Woman'.[1] The Luwian rituals, especially those from Hupesna, Istanuwa, and Lallupiya,[2] contain some names of deities, but for the most part these seem never to have been integrated into the Hittite pantheon. Exceptions are Yarri and Sanda, both gods of war and pestilence armed with a bow,[3] and the Sun-god Tiwat.[4] Sanda, concealed under the logogram Marduk, already appears among the divine witnesses in Suppiluliuma's treaty with Hukkana; Yarri in his treaties with Šattiwaza and Tette. The group of deities with names containing the element -sipa, viz. Kamrusepa, Askasipa, Ispanzasipa, Huriyanzipa, Hilanzipa, Hantasipa, Miyatanzipa, Suwanzipa, and Tarsanzipa, should probably also be regarded as Luwian in origin;[5] but of these only Kamrusepa, a beneficent patroness of healing and magic, has a recognizable personality.[6]

It is quite otherwise with the Hurrian pantheon. Hurro-Mesopotamian deities such as Ea, Ishtar of Nineveh (with Ninatta and Kulitta), and Allatum already appear in treaty lists from the reign of Suppiluliuma, though here the Akkadogram Allatum, the name for the queen of the Underworld, probably stands for Lelwani, the Hattian male counterpart, who underwent a sex-change under the influence of Akkadian theology.[7] In Syria, as we have seen, Allatum was held to be the

[1] Haas and Wilhelm, 1974, *passim*.

[2] *CTH* 690–4, 771, 772–3.

[3] Yarri is *bēl qašti* 'lord of the bow' and a regular helper in war for Mursili II (Goetze, 1933b, *passim*); see also Goetze, 1957, 134; Laroche, 1966, 291; and Kümmel, 1967, 101 ff., who traces a connection with the Babylonian Erra and with Apollo as archer. He appears in the Luwian ritual from Istanuwa, *CTH* 772.1, as well as in *CTH* 764, a Luwian ritual which seems to have a rather mixed pantheon. On Sanda see Laroche, 1973, 108 ff., comparing Herakles as a god, and below, pp. 29–30.

[4] Laroche, 1959, 128.

[5] These names were discussed by Laroche, 1946/7, 67 ff. and Goetze, 1953, 265 f. (for Miyatanzipa, cf. Otten and von Soden, 1968, 15, and for Tarsanzipa, possibly to be read Hassanzipa, Otten, 1971, 24 and 40). Goetze concluded that the suffix *-sipa* 'creates in one of the Anatolian languages adjectives of appurtenance, (and) this is certainly neither Hittite nor Luwian', but for Laroche it means 'spirit, daemon' (hardly the same as the word *šipa-* denoting a disease or symptom, Burde, 1974, 34, Otten, 1942, 41 n. 3). Kamrusepa and Askasepa are among the deities celebrated by the 'singer of Kanesh', but they are not attested in the Old Assyrian texts or in the Old Kingdom, and Kamrusepa at least is found mainly in texts of a Luwian or Kizzuwadnean character (Haas, 1971, 419 ff.; Haas and Wilhelm, 1974, 24). On the other hand, Hilanzipa belongs to the Palaic pantheon (Kammenhuber, 1959, 32 and 75), and the first element in most of these names is Hittite (*aška-* 'gate', *išpant-* 'night', *hila-* 'court', etc.).

[6] See Lecture III, p. 54; Haas, 1971, 419 ff.; Haas and Wilhelm, 1974, 24 ff.

[7] Otten, 1950, 129; Kammenhuber, 1972, 299.

mother of Hebat, but in the treaty lists the two are quite distinct. It seems that the conquests of Suppiluliuma introduced Hurrian deities to cult-centres west of the Taurus, and in the Hukkana treaty we already find Hebat installed at Kummanni and Uda, whilst Kubaba, previously the local goddess of Carchemish, appears to have a cult in Hattusa itself by the time of Muwatalli.[1]

In the thirteenth century, when Hattusili married the priestess of Kizzuwadna, Puduhepa, the Hurrian gods of Kummanni virtually took over the State religion.[2] At their head stood the national Weather-god Teshub and his queen Hebat, with two local deities, Sarruma and Allanzu, as their son and daughter.[3] Teshub was worshipped in the form of a bull (Plate III) and Sarruma, originally the genius of a local mountain, received the title 'Teshub's calf'. But in this pantheon, for purposes of sacrifice, the gods and goddesses were more or less segregated into two distinct series, called *kalutis*.[4] In broad outline, the list of gods begins with Teshub and a small group of associates, consisting of his brother Tasmisu, the elder god Kumarbi, a deity Suwaliyat whose character is unclear, and a god concealed under the logogram NINURTA. The order of these is variable. Then follow Ea, Kusuh the Moon-god, Simegi the Sun-god, the group Astabi, Lupatig (or Nupatig), and Hesui, who seem to combine between them in some way the characters of War-god (ZABABA), 'KAL' and god of pestilence (NERGAL);[5] the male form of Ishtar-Sausga, another related deity Pirinkir, Tenu the vizier of Teshub, the Sky and the Earth. At the end come the attendants of Teshub, including his son Sarruma 'the calf of Teshub', the bulls Seri and Hurri,[6] and the mountains Namni and Hazzi (the latter being the Syrian Mons Casius, the modern Jebel el Akra).

The corresponding *kaluti* of goddesses begins with Hebat, together with her son Sarruma and her daughter Allanzu. Thus Sarruma appears in both series. This list shows a grouping of names by pairs, and in conformity with this scheme Sarruma and Allanzu are both paired with their mother. The next pair, Darru–Dakitu, appears similarly to denote a single deity, Dakitu, perhaps Semitic 'the little one', a servant of Hebat in the mythology.[7] Then come Hutena–Hutellura, Hurrian names based on

[1] See above, p. 6 (from *CTH* 381).
[2] Laroche, 1948b, *passim*; 1952, 121 f.; Kammenhuber, 1974, 158.
[3] Laroche, 1963, 298 ff.
[4] Laroche, 1948b, *passim*; 1952, 118; Güterbock, 1961a.
[5] Cf. Otten, 1959a; Güterbock, 1961a, 11; Kammenhuber, 1975.
[6] On these bulls see now Haas, 1975a.
[7] Laroche, 1968, 503; Danmanville, 1975, 327.

a verb *ḫute-* 'to write'.[1] These were goddesses of fate and were equated with the Hittite divinities whose names are written enigmatically Gulses and MAḪ.MEŠ. After much discussion it is now at least clear that these were goddesses of individual destiny, presiding at birth and acting as nurses, also in mythology creatresses of man.[2] As already mentioned, the Hattian counterparts were Istustaya and Papaya,[3] though there is no evidence that the identification was ever made. Ishhara follows here, the ancient Mesopotamian goddess, regarded by the Hittites as guardian of the oath and also as bearer of a fatal disease,[4] and Allani 'the Lady', a title of the Queen of the Underworld, Erishkigal or Allatum.[5] Next come Nikkal, the Sumerian Ningal who had a popular cult at Kummanni as wife of the Moon-god Kusuh,[6] and 'Ishtar', here the great Hurrian goddess Sausga, with her attendants Ninatta and Kulitta. Among the minor goddesses who follow we recognize Naparbi, wife of Suwaliyat,[7] Šaluš, wife of Kumarbi (and formerly of Dagan),[8] and Kubaba, the goddess of Carchemish, who was to attain preeminence centuries later as Kybebe-Cybele, the Great Mother of Phrygian religion.[9]

This pantheon confronts us in countless rituals of the later period and in prayers uttered by Queen Puduhepa. By a process of syncretism the Hurrian divinities were to some extent identified with their Hattian and Hittite counterparts, a well-known example being the prayer of Puduhepa which contains the following passage:

> O Sun-goddess of Arinna, my lady, queen of all the countries, in the land of Hatti thou bearest the name 'Sun-goddess of Arinna', but in the country which thou hast made the land of cedars thou bearest the name 'Hebat'.[10]

Alternatively, they might be simply juxtaposed, as in the festival in honour of Sausga of Samuha, where we find the Sun-goddess of Arinna and her daughter Mezulla followed by Hebat, Sarruma and the whole Hurrian *kaluti* in a single series.[11]

[1] Laroche, 1948b, 124 ff.; Haas, 1975b.

[2] Most recently, Carruba, 1966, 29 ff., 34 ff.; Otten–Siegelova, 1970; Otten, 1975.

[3] Above, p. 12.

[4] As guardian of the oath, Kümmel, 1967, 38; as bearer of a fatal disease, Burde, 1974, 12–16. Cf. also Laroche, 1974, 180.

[5] See above, p. 5 n. 6.

[6] *CTH* 381. i. 63; Laroche, 1955a, 12; 1966, 349.

[7] Laroche, 1948b, 128; Güterbock, 1961a, 15. Possibly in origin '(goddess) of Nippur' (Laroche, loc. cit.); cf. Kumarbi (p. 14).

[8] Laroche, 1948b, 122, 132; 1968, 524.

[9] Laroche, 1960a.

[10] *ANET* 393.

[11] *CTH* 712. ii. 36 ff.; Laroche, 1948b, 123.

Hattusili III adopted Sausga of Samuha as his personal deity; but at the same time he appears to have encouraged an active Hattian revival. The holy city Nerik had been overrun many centuries earlier by the barbarian Kaska folk and the cult of its Weather-god had been carried on at the neighbouring city of Hakpis.[1] Hattusili tells us with pride that he recaptured the place and restored its cults. Now Nerik was an ancient Hattian centre and the newly reconstructed rituals and myths of Nerik are concerned with Hattian deities. Many even contain passages in Hattic with Hittite translation. It is not always easy to distinguish these late texts from those of the Old Kingdom with their predominantly Hattian colouring.[2] The chief god of Nerik was its Weather-god, who was identified with the Weather-god of Zippalanda and also to some extent with the Hurrian Sarruma, as son of the Weather-god of Hatti. Other local gods were the Mountain Zaliyanu and his spouse Zashapuna. Sulinkatte (= Nergal) and the War-god Wurunkatte also enjoyed a cult at Nerik.[3]

That the Hurrian religion finally prevailed may be seen most clearly in the sculptures of Yazilikaya, the open-air shrine near Boğazköy (frontispiece), which date from the time of Tudhaliya IV, Hattusili's son and successor. Tudhaliya's chosen personal god was Sarruma who, as we have seen, ranked low among the Hurrian gods and was regarded as a junior attached to his mother. Yazilikaya is faithful to the Hurrian conception, though in the smaller chamber, to which we shall return in the second lecture, this god is depicted again in heroic proportions as the patron of the king (Plate II).

In the main chamber we see depicted in relief on the walls the two *kalutis* of Teshub and Hebat in the form of two processions meeting at the central point (Fig. 1). In the last ten years much progress has been made in reading the badly weathered hieroglyphic signs forming the names of the deities, and most of them can now be identified.[4] On the wall facing the entrance (Plate I*a*) are Teshub and Hebat with their son and daughter, Sarruma and Allanzu, and their granddaughter.[5] For reasons

[1] Haas, 1970, 7, and *passim*. [2] Kammenhuber, 1972, 293. [3] Haas, op. cit., 67 ff.

[4] Laroche, 1969, *passim*; the latest exposition is by Güterbock in Bittel, 1975.

[5] According to Laroche, *both* the figures standing on the double-headed eagle represent the daughter, Allanzu; but Güterbock would read the legend by the right-hand figure (no. 46) as 'Granddaughter of Teshub' (loc. cit. 172). In the Hattian pantheon the supreme pair, the Weather-god Taru and the Sun-goddess of Arinna, had a granddaughter whose name, Zintuhi, is simply the Hattian word for 'granddaughter'. The fact that at Yazilikaya this goddess bears not a name but a logographic description shows that in Hurrian there was no equivalent and that the artist was deliberately 'translating' the Hattian pantheon.

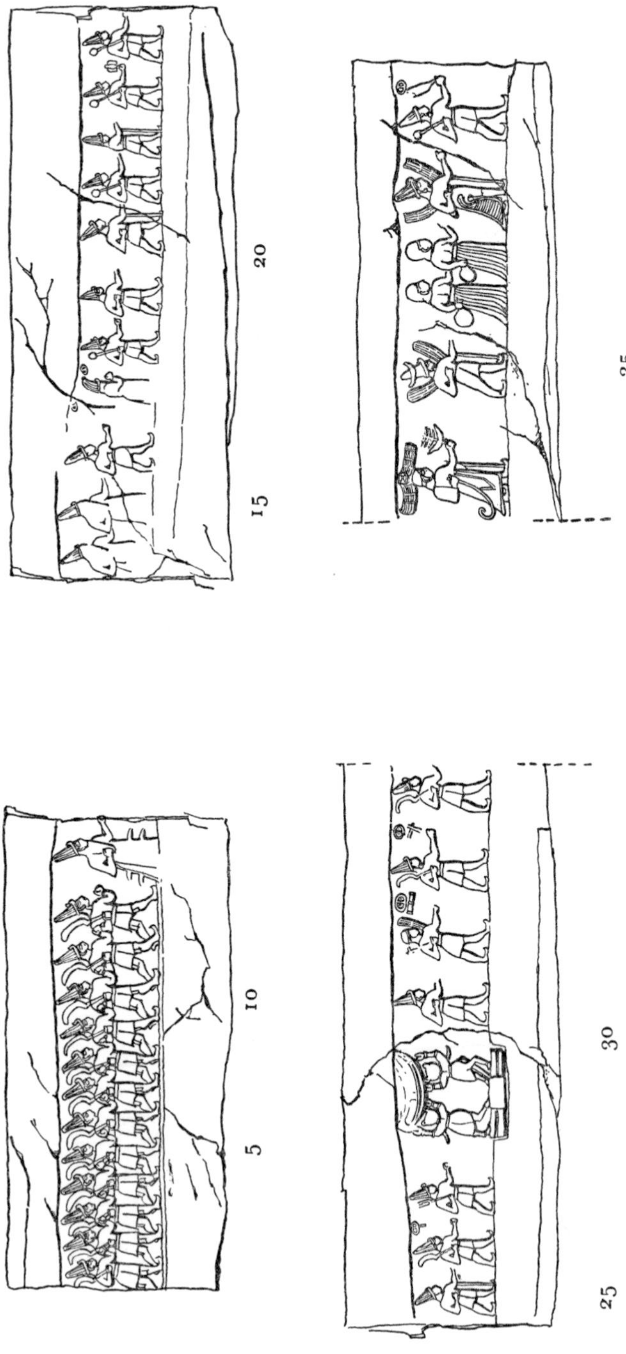
15
20
35
5
10
25
30

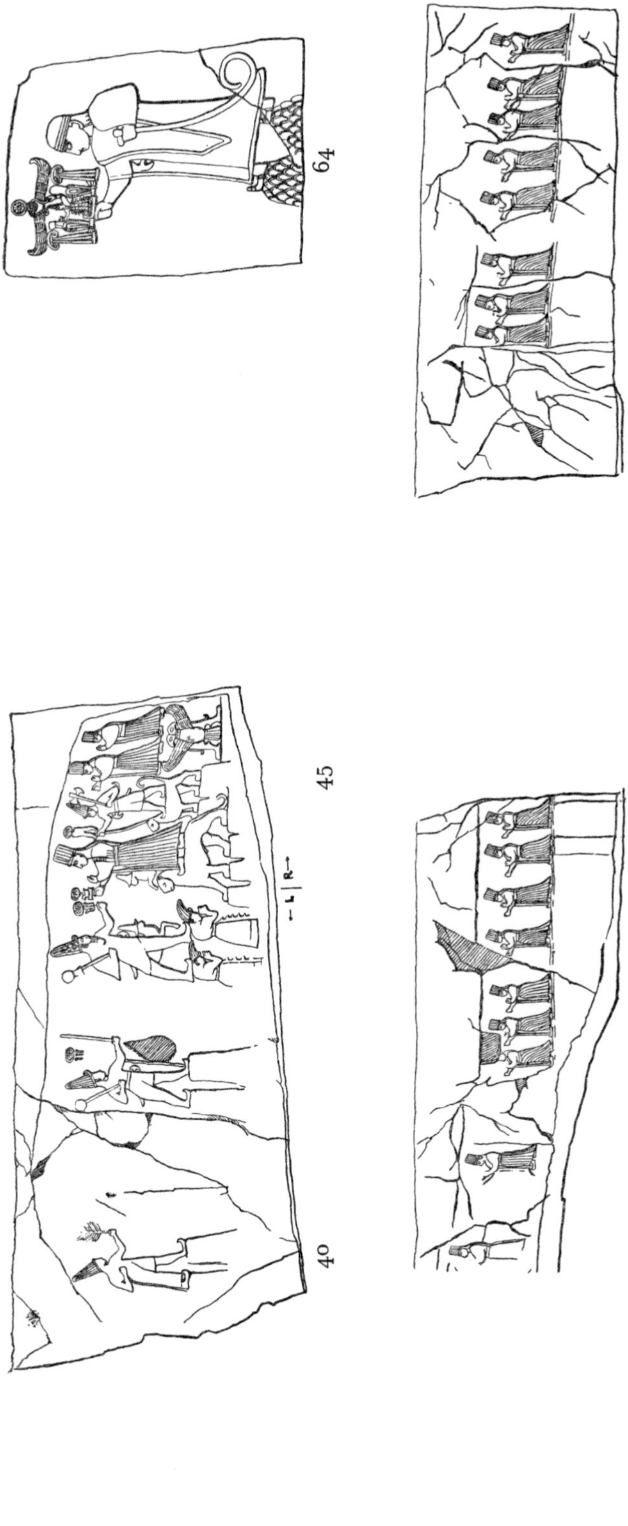

Fig. 1. Yazilikaya. The sculptures of Chamber A

at present unknown, the artist has shown Hebat and Sarruma standing on panthers and Allanzu and the granddaughter standing on a double-headed eagle; and he has also represented Sarruma as the 'calf of Teshub' a second time, and moreover twice, by the legs of each of his parents. Teshub stands on mountain gods, exactly as described in a passage of a cult-inventory:

> Weather-god of Heaven, a male statue, plated with gold, in his right hand he holds a club, in his left hand he holds a golden symbol of good, standing on two mountains in the form of male statues plated with silver.[1]

The procession following Teshub consists of forty-one deities (Plate I*b*), of whom the names of the following can be read with certainty:

No. 39: Ea.
No. 38: Sauska
No. 35: MOON
No. 34: SUN of HEAVEN
No. 33: Astabi
No. 32: ANTLER-ti (= ^{d}KAL)

In the *kaluti* of Teshub, as already mentioned, Ea, the Moon-god, the Sun-god, Astabi, and a 'tutelary' god of the KAL type are listed in just this order, and Ishtar-Sausga—the male form of this deity—is included, though at a later point. The two gods nos. 41 and 40, between Teshub and Ea, should according to the lists be two of the group consisting of Teshub's brother Tasmisu and the gods Suwaliyat and Kumarbi. If Suwaliyat is merely another name for Tasmisu, as has been thought, there is no further difficulty here: no. 41 is the 'brother of Teshub', no. 40 is Kumarbi,[2] The two small girls following Sausga (nos. 37 and 36), both of whose names can be seen to end in *-tá*, must be her attendants Ninatta and Kulitta. For nos. 31 and 30 Pirinkir and Hesui have been suggested. The two signs combined in a single design with a pair of bull-men, nos. 29–8, represent heaven and earth, and the bull-men, who are nameless, could be Seri and Hurri. The remainder are uncertain, but nos. 17–13 are depicted as mountain-gods and appear to be labelled 'divine mountains'. The twelve runners who bring up the rear

[1] Brandenstein, 1943, 6, 8–11; the description differs only in that the statue described was 'sitting', whereas at Yazilikaya (and similarly at Imamkulu, Bossert, 1942, 563) the deity is standing. Cf. Güterbock, op. cit. 189.

[2] Identifications proposed by Laroche and accepted by Güterbock, though the actual reading of the signs is uncertain.

may be the 'twelve gods of the crossroads', a group once mentioned in association with the Underworld god Nergal.[1]

In the female procession, both the figures and the names are badly damaged. There were originally twenty goddesses following Allanzu and the granddaughter, but one has been totally obliterated and at least one, more probably two, have been cut out and removed elsewhere. One of the latter was found at the neighbouring village of Yekbas.[2]

The name of the defaced goddess, no. 46a, is now illegible, but by a judicious use of the drawings made by nineteenth-century travellers Laroche has restored the name as Dakitu 'the little one', with the possibility that it is to be read in its enigmatic compounded form Darru-Dakitu.[3] Nos. 47 and 48 can be identified with certainty as Hutena-Hutellura, the Hurrian goddesses of fate. No. 49 is read *A-la-tu*, i.e. Allatum, corresponding to Allani in the lists, Ishhara being omitted. Nos. 50 and 52 are nameless, no. 51 is uncertain, but no. 53 is read *Tá-pa-ki-na*, i.e. Damkina, the wife of Ea, and no. 54 is Nikkal (Ningal), the wife of the Moon-god. The relief found at Yekbas shows a goddess without a name, but behind her is written quite clearly the name Sausga, which presumably belongs to a second missing figure.[4] Thus, just as in the lists, Ishtar-Sausga appears in both processions. It is rather strange that the attendants, Ninatta and Kulitta, have been put in the male procession, but they are carved in a way which suggests that they may have been a later addition.[5] The rest of this procession is unidentified.

The nature and purpose of this rock shrine will be discussed in the next lecture. The reliefs were probably executed for Tudhaliya IV, whose figure is carved on a rock facing the central group. Their almost exact correspondence with the Hurrian *kalutis* strikingly demonstrates the dominance of the Hurrian elements in the State religion by the end of the thirteenth century.

[1] Güterbock, 1964, 72 n. 91; 1965, 198; and *apud* Bittel, 1975, 191–2.

[2] Güterbock, 1947, 189 ff. Alternative positions for this block are discussed in Bittel, 1975, 114 f. It is illustrated in Vieyra, 1955, pl. 23; Laroche, 1969, 98.

[3] Doubts are expressed about this reading by Güterbock *apud* Bittel, 1975, 180.

[4] Vieyra, 1955, 64; Danmanville, 1962, 14; Güterbock *apud* Bittel, 1975, 181.

[5] Bittel, 1941, 70; 1975, 140; Beran, 1965, 269–70.

THE DEITIES OF YAZILIKAYA

Central group:

No. 42: Teshub
No. 42a: 'Calf of Teshub' (= Sarruma)
No. 43: Hebat
No. 44: Sarruma
No. 45: Allanzu
No. 46: 'Teshub's grandchild'

Left side:

No. 41: 'Brother of Teshub'(?)
No. 40: Kumarbi
No. 39: Ea
No. 38: Sausga
No. 37: Ninatta
No. 36: Kulitta
No. 35: 'Moon-god'
No. 34: 'Sun-god of Heaven'
No. 33: Astabi
No. 32: 'Stag-god' (KAL)
No. 31: Pirinkir(?)
No. 30: Hesui
No. 29–8: Seri and Hurri
No. 27: Nergal(?)
No. 26: Pisaisaphi
Rest either nameless or illegible.

Right side:

No. 46a: Darru-Dakitu
No. 47: Hutena
No. 48: Hutellura
No. 49: Allatu
No. 51: Naparbi(?)
No. 52: Šaluš-Bitinhi(?)[1]
No. 53: Tapkina (= Damkina)
No. 54: Nikkal (= Ningal)
No. 55: Aya(?)[1]
No. 55a (Yekbas figure): nameless
No. 55b (Yekbas name): Sausga
Rest illegible.

[1] Haas and Wäfler, 1974, 220; Güterbock, 1975b, 276.

II

THE CULT

Religious texts form a large proportion of the Hittite royal library. Out of the 20,000 fragments recovered since excavations started in 1907, some 600 distinct works have been identified, and of these about 170 are religious. Even so, comparison with the titles listed in the ancient catalogues shows that only about one seventh of the original library has been recovered.[1] The religious texts fall into the categories of myths, prayers and hymns, festivals and ceremonies, cult inventories, divination reports, and magical rituals. I propose to deal in this lecture with the cult inventories and some of the festival texts, which provide our main evidence for the religious cults.

Knowledge of the age-old local cults comes almost entirely from the cult inventories.[2] These appear to be reports of commissioners sent out by King Tudhaliya IV, late in the thirteenth century B.C., to collect information about the condition of the shrines in the various regions.[3] Many of them are mere lists of temple furniture, though these often record recent donations made by the king for the enrichment of the shrine. Others are more elaborate and include descriptions of the local religious festivals. Some of these texts are particularly well preserved, and they have been well edited by C. W. Carter in a Chicago dissertation.[4]

We find—rather surprisingly—that in most of these shrines cult-images in human form were an innovation due to the king's benefaction. Formerly the deity had been represented either by a symbol or by a stela, for which the Hittite word is '*ḫuwaši* stone'. The exception is the Weather-god, who in most instances was represented by a *bull*, both before and after the enrichment of the shrine, just as we see him represented on the well-known sculpture at Alaca Hüyük (Plate III). Thus at a place called Marash (not the same as modern Maraş) there were four deities. Originally the Weather-god had been in the form of a bull, tin-plated, standing on all fours; the second, a

[1] Laroche, 1971, 192–3.
[2] *CTH* 501–30; cf. von Brandenstein, 1943; Jakob-Rost, 1963.
[3] Laroche, 1975, 91. Cf. Carter, 1962, 17 ff. [4] Carter, 1962.

mountain god, had been represented by a weapon (^{giš}TUKUL), possibly a mace; the third by five copper daggers; and the fourth by a stela showing a mother suckling her child. These were replaced respectively by a silver bull, a mace adorned with a sun-disc and a moon-crescent and surmounted by an iron figure of a man, a silver figure of a standing man with eyes of gold holding a copper dagger, and a figure of a woman suckling her child.[1] At Hursalassi the Weather-god had been represented by a *wakšur* vessel, which was replaced by an iron bull; the goddess Haburiyata had been in the form of a stela, which was replaced by a figure of a seated woman.[2] Conversely, at Wattarwa a tin-plated figure of the Weather-god was replaced by a bull.[3] Only in five places are anthropomorphic figures of the Weather-god attested, though this seems to have been a general rule for other deities.[4] Objects donated by the king were often inscribed with his name. At Tahurpa during a festival the queen offered sacrifices to eight Sun-goddesses of Arinna in the form of three statues and five sun-discs, which had apparently been donated by six of her predecessors, and presumably bore their names.[5]

For the most part these images do not appear to have been life-sized statues. Their size is given in the inventories in terms of the unit *šekan*, which has been determined as about 22 cm., just under 9 inches.[6] They measure for the most part either 1 or 1½ *šekan*, occasionally 2 *šekan*, that is, *c.* 9–18 inches. Thus they are definitely statuettes, not statues. Such statuettes have been found.[7] Yet scenes of worship generally show life-sized cult-images, and Bittel has pointed out that the size of the bases in the excavated temples at the capital proves that there at least the cult-images must have been full-sized statues.[8] He therefore thinks that the statuettes were replicas. In fact we do not have inventories for the temples of the capital and they may well have had full-sized statues, probably of precious metal, if we may judge from a prayer of Puduhepa in which she vows to make for the goddess Lelwani 'a statue of Hattusili as big as Hattusili, with head, hands and feet of gold' if the goddess will preserve his health.[9] But the cult-inventories from the provincial towns say nothing of large statues and seem to indicate that in these places the statuettes were the actual cult-images.

1 *KBo.* II. 1. i. 28 ff. (*CTH* 509); Carter, 52, 61.
2 Ibid. ii. 32 ff.; Carter, 55, 64.
3 Ibid. ii. 21 ff.; Carter, 54, 64.
4 Jakob-Rost, 1963, 206.
5 *KUB* XXV. 14. i. 10–31; Gurney, 1958, 120; Bin-Nun, 1975, 197 ff.
6 Jakob-Rost, 1963, 176–8; Alp, 1961/2, 233.
7 Cf. Alp, 1961/2; Bittel, 1964, 123 ff.
8 Bittel, 1964, 126.
9 *ANET* 394.

The festivals described in these texts take place mainly in spring and autumn, and we learn that in most cult-centres the deity had a stela or *ḫuwaši*-stone set up not only in his temple but also in a locality outside the town, in the open country, usually by a grove or a spring, or on a mountain. In such cases they are often said to be in a structure called a *tarnu*-house, which may be nothing more than a temenos wall.[1] One of these festivals, which has been frequently quoted, is the following:

When it is the time for the autumn festival of the Weather-god, they wash, the priest carries the god to the *ḫuwaši*-stone, they wash the *ḫuwaši*-stone and anoint it. They put down the god in front of the *ḫuwaši*-stone. The priest offers one sheep for Yarri and one sheep for the Seven Gods. They slaughter them at the *ḫuwaši*. They set meat (various loaves of bread) and a vessel of beer, for the cult-stand. They break bread and fill the rhytons. They eat, they drink, the *ḫazgara*-women entertain the god. They divide the young men into two groups and name them; one group they call 'men of Hatti', the other group they call 'men of Masa'. The men of Hatti have bronze weapons, but the men of Masa have weapons of reed. And they fight, and the men of Hatti win. They take a prisoner of war and devote him to the god. Then they pick up the god and carry him back to the temple and put him on the cult-stand. They break bread, offer beer and erect the lamps.[2]

Here is a second example:

When it becomes spring and it thunders . . . the priests . . . carry the mountain-god Halwanna up to the mountain. Now if the area is controlled by the enemy, they carry him to the mountain and place him in front of the *ḫuwaši*-stone, which stands under a tree. They break bread and offer beer. But if the area is not controlled by the enemy, they set him by the *ḫuwaši* under the tree by the side of the river. They offer 1 ox and 8 sheep. They set down meat; bread and beer for the cult-stand and other bread and beer for display. . . . They eat and drink, they fill the cups. In the presence of the god there is wrestling. They start fighting, they make merry. When the sun sets they carry the god down to the city and set him up in the temple.[3]

A similar local festival in which the king takes part is the following:

The king goes into the inner room. . . . They bring the Sun-god down to the wood and put him (by) the *ḫuwaši*. They consecrate 1 fat ox and 7 sheep and slaughter them by the *ḫuwaši*.

When the king celebrates the Weather-god of the Army, he stands forward and consecrates a fat bull, 4 sheep (among them 1 lamb) and

[1] Darga, 1969, 13 n. 14.
[2] *KUB* XVII. 35. iii. 1 ff.; Carter, 1962, 129, 142. Cf. Ehelolf, 1925; Lesky, 1927.
[3] *KUB* XXV. 23. i. 8 ff.; Carter, 154, 164.

4 goats (among them 1 kid). They slaughter them at the *ḫuwaši*. . . . (All this) in one day in the forest of Anziliya.[1]

These festivals consist regularly of sacrifice, feasting, and an entertainment (*duškaraz*).[2] There could be no better illustration of the type of religion described by Robertson Smith in 1888:

> Everywhere we find that a sacrifice ordinarily involves a feast and that a feast cannot be provided without a sacrifice. For a feast is not complete without flesh, and in early times the rule that all slaughter is sacrifice was not confined to the Semites. . . . When men meet their god they feast and are glad together, and whenever they feast and are glad they desire that the god should be of the party.[3]

In these rather concise texts the procedure of sacrifice is described briefly in two stages, denoted by the verbs *šipant-* and *ḫuek-*. The first action is performed by the priest, the second by the indefinite 'they' or by the cook. The verb *šipant-*, which is cognate with Greek σπένδω, is the verb used for pouring libations. For this reason, when used of an animal, it has been thought to refer to the shedding of the blood and is sometimes translated 'brings as a blood-sacrifice'.[4] However, Goetze has now shown that there are passages in which the animal remains alive and apparently unharmed after this action,[5] and in more detailed descriptions of sacrifice we find that the blood is only shed after the second action, denoted by *ḫuek-* or *ḫatta-*, both approximately 'to slaughter'. I am therefore adopting Goetze's translation 'to consecrate' for *šipant-*. That there was some difference between *ḫuek-* and *ḫatta-* is shown by the following passage from a ritual against impotence:

> Then I consecrate a sheep to Uliliassi and they slaughter it (*ḫuek-*) down in front of the table. Finally they remove the sheep, cut it up(?) (*ḫatta-*) and [cook] it.[6]

Usually, however, only one of these two verbs is found—indeed both may be omitted and *šipant-* left to stand for the whole procedure in the sense 'to sacrifice'.

Blood indeed plays very little part in Hittite sacrifice, just as in ancient Mesopotamia. The text which has been quoted in

[1] *CTH* 681; Dinçol and Darga, 1969/70, 105, 19 ff., and 107, 15 ff.

[2] Carter, 67 f.; Güterbock, 1964, 72.

[3] Smith, 1901, 255. This is the communion sacrifice (*zeḇah šelāmîm*) of the O.T. which is thought to be part of a pre-Semitic heritage (Rost, 1958; de Vaux, 1964).

[4] Otten, 1958a, 126 f.; 1961b, 129 (3), 131 (32); 1971, 5 (38); Haas-Wilhelm, 1974, *passim*. Cf. Kümmel, 1973a, 347.

[5] Goetze, 1970/1, 88. For the ritual of Zarpiya (see below) the point was already made by Schwartz, 1938, 347.

[6] Ritual of Paskuwatti, *CTH* 406, *ANET* 350. For 'slaughtering down' see p. 30 n. 4.

support of the translation 'brings as a blood-sacrifice' is in fact unique and has a different terminology:

The chief cook 'cuts' (*kuirzi*) 10 sheep and 2 oxen to the Weather-god by the hearth. . . . And he occupies himself with(?) the blood of the sheep, and he keeps libating the blood in front of the cult-stand.[1]

This text belongs to the cult of the royal ancestors and the reason for the emphasis on blood here is not clear. In view of the countless examples with the normal terminology where there is no reference to blood, it is doubtful whether this passage should be taken as revealing the true meaning of the verb *šipant-*.

In other passages where blood is mentioned there are special reasons. It was a regular offering for the chthonic deities, who craved for it,[2] as in the following passage from the invocation of the Underworld gods to absolve a house from blood-guilt:

The water which he has brought from the spring he libates into the water(?). Then he consecrates (*šipant-*) a lamb with the water (var. into the water). They slaughter (*ḫatta-*) it and let the blood run into a clay *ḫuppar* vessel and place it before the God of Blood (this is an image which has just been made), and he says: 'Anunnaki, whatever blood-guilt is in (this house), take it and give it to the God of Blood, let him take it down to the dark Underworld and there peg it down fast.'[3]

The blood of the victim here is not only an offering to the Underworld gods but also a symbol of the blood-guilt infecting the house.

In the ritual of Zarpiya blood functions as part of the symbolism of sharing a meal in order to establish a covenant relationship with a deity:

They lead in a goat and the master of the house consecrates (*šipant-*) the goat in front of the table to Sanda with wine. Then he holds out a bronze axe and says: 'Come, Sanda, and let the Violent Gods come with you, who are clothed in blood-stained garments and girt with the cords(?) of Lulahhi men, who have a dagger in the belt, draw bows and

[1] *KUB* X. 11. vi. 1–7, *CTH* 660, quoted by Otten, 1958a, 126, and Goetze, 1970/1, 85.

[2] Hoffner, 1967a, 395; McCarthy, 1969, 171 ff.

[3] *CTH* 446; Otten, 1961b, 129. In line 3 Otten prefers the variant *ú-e-te-ni* (*KBo* X. 45. iii. 12) and translates 'makes a blood-sacrifice into the water'. But the repetition of *weteni(t) šipanti* is suspect and the text appears to be corrupt. Water has been specially brought from a spring. It hardly makes sense to say that it is then 'libated into the water', or that the lamb is slaughtered 'into it'. It is more likely to have been brought for purposes of purification; and the verb *šipanti* belongs properly to the lamb. In favour of the textual reading A-*e-te-ni-it* BAL-*ti* (*KUB* XLI. 8. iii. 3) is the closely parallel *IŠ-TU* GEŠTIN *ši-pa-an-ti* of the Zarpiya ritual (below).

The 'Anunnaki' are the Primeval Gods of the Hurrians described above, p. 15.

hold arrows. Come and eat! And we will take the oath.' When he has finished speaking he puts the bronze axe down on the table and they slaughter (*ḫatta-*) the goat. He takes the blood and smears the drinking tube which is inserted into the tankard with the blood. They bring the raw liver and the heart and the master of the house offers them to the god and takes a bite. They do an imitation(?). Then he puts his lip to the tube and sips and says: 'Behold, Sanda and Violent Gods, we have taken oath. Since we have bitten the raw liver and drunk from one(?) tube, therefore Sanda and Violent Ones, do not again approach my gate.' Then they cook the liver and heart with fire and cut up all the rest of the goat. . . . He takes the shoulder and breast. . . . Then they surround the table and eat up the shoulder and breast. Then [just as they wish(?)] to eat and drink, so he brings, and they eat [up(?) . . .] and they drink [. . .] the tankard.[1]

This passage has been strangely neglected in the controversy over the significance of the West Semitic custom of killing an animal to sanctify a covenant or treaty.[2] It is the clearest expression of the belief in the efficacy of this solemn rite, which at Mari and at Alalakh was virtually synonymous with the covenant itself, and still had its full force in the covenant of Moses (Exod. 24: 5–8). In the first millennium its original significance had apparently been forgotten and the slaughter of the victim was used merely as one among many analogical warnings of the fate awaiting the transgressor.

Hoffner has pointed out that the Greeks killed the sacrificial animal with the throat upwards for the Olympians and with the throat downwards for the Chthonians (so that the blood might more easily soak into the earth), but he remarks that the Hittite texts make no mention of the position of the animal's throat.[3] It may perhaps be suggested that this is the significance of the distinction between 'slaughtering up' and 'slaughtering down' which has puzzled commentators.[4] But this would need further investigation.

[1] *CTH* 757, translated by Schwartz, 1938. See Gurney, 1940, 64 and Laroche, 1973, 110. The ritual is of Luwian origin and is for the purpose of ridding the country of an epidemic caused by Sanda (written MARDUK) and his bloodthirsty associates the Innarawantes. On Sanda see above, p. 16. Though an offering of blood might be thought appropriate to this group, it is not in fact offered, but is used to establish a mystical bond between the wine which is drunk by the participants and the victim which is shared with the god. The offering of the entrails to the god, while the participants consume the rest of the meat, may be compared to the Hebrew practice as laid down in Lev. 3 and 7. Cf. p. 56 n. 3.

For *ḫimma-* 'model, imitation' see now Oettinger, 1976, 61 ff. Since models are not used in this ritual, 'they' must be presumed to imitate the householder's actions.

[2] Discussed at length by McCarthy, 1963, 52 ff.

[3] Hoffner, 1967a, 399.

[4] 'Slaughtering down' (*katta/kattanda ḫuek-/hatta-*) is the expression commonly used when the blood is shed into a pit of some sort (*ḫattešni, pattešni, api, ANA* TÚL, *wappui*) for the *dei inferi* (e.g. Haas, 1970, 142, 4; Otten, 1961b, 120, 42; Otten, 1958a, 58, 5; *KUB* X. 63. i. 15,

Turning from the local to the national cult, we are confronted by a great mass of texts forming the bulk of the Hittite library. The public rituals are the festivals (EZEN),[1] particularly those in which the king takes part. There are at least eighty names for such festivals,[2] but to judge from their duration (so far as it is known) the most important were once again those held in the spring and the autumn. The spring festival was named after the AN.TAḪ.ŠUM plant, possibly the crocus or saffron, and lasted 38 days; the plant was 'taken' by the king and queen (whatever that may mean) on the 9th day.[3] The autumn festival was called *nuntariyašḫaš* and lasted at least 21 days.[4] The KI.LAM festival, also held in the spring, had at least eleven tablets,[5] and the *ḫisuwa* or *isuwa* festival (a late arrival from a Hurrian milieu) thirteen, though days are not mentioned.[6] Another spring festival was the *purulli* festival, to which we shall return. It had at least thirty-two tablets.[7] It is typical of the autumn festivals that the storage vessels are filled and at the spring festivals the same vessels are opened and their contents used.[8]

In the festival texts the performance of the ceremonies is described in great detail, so that a whole tablet is usually assigned to the rites of a single day. These ceremonies are all very similar and since most of the tablets are fragmentary it is difficult to distinguish one festival from another. The distinctive character of each festival will not be understood until more tablets have been identified and placed in their proper sequence. As an example we may take the tablet for the sixteenth day of the AN.TAḪ.ŠUM festival, which has often been quoted on account of its comparatively good preservation, though the tablet in fact describes only the second half of the day's ritual and the first half is missing. This day's celebrations are in honour of the War-god, Wurunkatte.[9]

20; XXIX. 4. iv. 36; *KBo* XI. 14. iii. 9; 17. ii. 14). But what is 'slaughtering up'? e.g. [GIŠ]*eyani šarā ḫukanzi*, *KUB* XXV. 33. i. 8; *šarā ANA* NINDA.KUR.$_4$RA.ḪI.A *ḫukanzi*, *IBoT* I. 29. i. 42; [GIŠ]*laḫḫurnuzziaš šarā ḫukanzi*, Sturtevant–Bechtel, 1935, 110, 36. Cf. Friedrich, *HWb*. 70 s.v. *ḫuek-*. In the last two examples Goetze (1970/1, 90) translates 'on'. But this would be *šer*, not *šarā*.

[1] Cf. Güterbock, 1969, 175.
[2] They are listed by Hoffner, 1967b, 39 ff.
[3] Güterbock, 1960a; 1964, 62 ff.; *CTH* 604–25.
[4] *CTH* 626; Güterbock, 1964, 68 f.; Laroche, 1972, no. 626, Bo. 2438.
[5] *CTH* 627; Güterbock, 1969, 178 f.
[6] *CTH* 628; Güterbock, ibid. 179 f.
[7] The catalogue *KUB* XXX. 42. i. 5 (*CTH* p. 162) lists the 32nd tablet (Haas, 1970, 43).
[8] Gurney, 1940, 121; Güterbock, 1964, 72; Hoffner, 1974, 49 f.
[9] *CTH* 612; *ANET* 358 ff. Cf. Güterbock, 1975a, 128.

The text opens in the first line with the call *waganna* 'to take a bite', the signal for the preparation of a cultic meal. Evidently, a sacrifice has already taken place, because after the king has left the temple and the place has been swept clean, the staff of the temple bring in the meat of a bull, and of cows, sheep, and goats and place it in front of the cult-stand before the god, and on either side of it two silver bowls for libation filled with wine. The king and queen go to the *ḫalentuwa* building (probably to be understood as the palace)[1], robe themselves, and proceed back to the temple to the accompaniment of music. After some purification ceremonies in the forecourt they enter the temple of the War-god. The king goes to the throne, while the queen enters the inner room. The chief cook brings portions of meat and puts them down by the hearth, by the throne, by the window, by the bolt of the door, and another again by the hearth. (These are known as the 'holy places'.) He then presents a libation vessel with wine to the king, and after the king has touched it with his hand, he pours libations, three before the throne, three for the god, one each for the same four holy places, and finally one for the statue of King Hattusili (probably Hattusili I). The king prostrates himself. The musicians leave. The king and queen now sit down on their thrones, and a palace servant brings in the 'lituus'[2] and places it at the king's right. There is further washing of hands. Now, the table is brought in and set up for the king. Various loaves and a pot-stand have been prepared outside. The princes, the senior cooks, and the priests are ushered in. The major-domo calls for 'music' and the musicians lift the 'Ishtar instruments' and carry them in, accompanied by various functionaries. The cooks serve meat and water. The *UBARU*-men[3] are brought in and seated and are served with *marnuwan*-beer.[4] The king and queen wash their hands and the sweepers sweep the floor. The cupbearer now gives the king some beer and he 'drinks to' the god Tauri;[5] the Ishtar instruments play, but there is no singing. The herald makes the congregation stand up. The king and queen standing 'drink to' the Sun-god and Tappinu[6] and the king pours a

[1] Güterbock, 1971, 307 ff.

[2] This is the long curved staff called *kalmuš* and held by the Hittite kings on numerous monuments (e.g. Plate I). Cf. Akurgal, 1962, 112; Garstang, 1929, 356; Alp, 1947.

[3] The part played by the *UBARU*-men in the temple cult is still not clear. Cf. Neu, 1970, 76–9.

[4] That *marnuwan* is a kind of beer has been shown by von Schuler, 1969.

[5] A Hattian deity, possibly a deified object or tree, since *KBo* II. 5. i. 2 has ^{giš}*ta-u-ri-ı* (Laroche, 1966, 253); but Kümmel, 1973b, 170 n. 6, regards this as a scribal error.

[6] Probably a name for the goddess Mezulla (Laroche, 1955c, 112).

libation while the musicians play and sing; he also breaks bread. He makes a gesture of reverence while standing. Now the king and queen sit down and a servant puts a linen cloth on their knees. The head palace servant announces twelve Arinna loaves to them, and the chief cook presents three pot-racks(?) beside the hearth. The king makes a gesture and they bring in *taḫtum-mara*.[1] The king and queen, sitting, 'drink to' the Weather-god of Zippalanda, while the musicians play. The king breaks a 'sour' loaf and a 'sweetened' loaf.[2] . . . The smiths bring two silver bulls' heads. These are filled with wine,[3] a priest pours a libation from them beside the hearth, and they take them out.[4] A 'table-man' takes a *tunnapta*-cake from the table and takes it out. Then the bulls' heads full of wine[5] and the *tunnapta*-cake are distributed.[6] The king and queen 'drink to' Hulla,[7] Telipinu,[8] and the War-god and the king breaks bread. The musicians play, and the congregation pays reverence to the king. The major-domo takes the cup-bearer's cloak. The cup-bearer holds a silver cup of wine and gives it to the king[9] and they withdraw backwards, keeping their eyes on the king and stand by the hearth. The major-domo lets go of the cup-bearer's cloak and the cup-bearer pays reverence to the king. The major-domo again takes hold of the cloak and brings him to the king.[10] The cup-bearer takes the cup from the king and the major-domo grasps him by his cloak on the left side. They go back to the hearth. A ZABAR.DIB man (butler) now comes in and takes the golden(!) cup with the wine from the cup-bearer and removes them. The 'kneelers' bring in certain foods and offer them to the king. The cup-bearer pays reverence to the king, picks up the bread and carries it out. The vergers make the congregation stand up. The palace servants take the knee-cloths from the king and queen. The king and queen stand up and 'drink to' the Sun-god to the accompaniment of music; he also breaks bread. The 'table-man' brings in a loaf and puts it by the window. The congregation remains standing. (Here the tablet ends, though the day is not yet finished.)

Comparing this with the simple ceremonies of the cult-inventories, we recognize the same elements: the sacrifices and libation, the cultic feast in which the congregation gets a share of food and drink after it has been blessed by the king, and the

[1] Probably an aromatic substance (Neu, 1970, 69 f.).
[2] Hoffner, 1974, 197, 199.
[3] Text restored from *KUB* XX. 83. iii. 5–8.
[4] Here *KUB* XXV. 1. iv. 31–5.
[5] *KUB* II. 5. iii. 25–6.
[6] Ibid. 30: *šar-[ra-an-zi]*.
[7] *IBoT* I. 20. iv. 10.
[8] *KUB* II. 5. iv. 12 = XXV. 1. v. 1 ff.
[9] *KUB* II. 5. v. 1 ff.
[10] *KUB* XXV. 1. v. 48 ff.

merry-making, now in the form of instrumental and vocal music. But the central act of the ritual, always performed by the king, is called literally 'drinking' the god.[1] In the early days of Hittitology it used to be assumed that in this phrase the verb 'drink' was used in a causative sense 'give to drink', the god being offered drink in the form of a libation (as illustrated on a relief from Malatya, Plate IV). Now comparison with the Old Hittite texts has shown that the phrase is an abbreviation. These old rituals have 'drink the cup of the god', an act usually performed by both the king and queen; the king alone then pours a libation. Later the cup was omitted and the god became the direct object of the verb, just as in these later texts the god occasionally appears as the direct object of the verb *šipant-*. The whole procedure is exactly like the medieval custom by which the host took a sip from the cup before offering it to his guest.

The musical instruments used in these rituals are the *arkammi*, the *galgalturi*, the *ḫuḫupal*, the *zinar* (with its two varieties *ḫunzinar*, and *ippizinar*), the *šawitra* or *šawatar*, and the *mukar*, together with four Sumerograms, GIŠ dINANNA, gisŠÀ.A.TAR, gisBALAG or BALAG.DI, and GI.GÍD. The GI.GÍD, literally 'long reed', is certainly a kind of flute or pipe, probably the double pipes shown on the monuments (e.g. Plates VI, VIII); and the *šawitra*, which is blown and has the determinative SI (horn) must be the horn (Plate V).[2] The logograms GIŠ dINANNA (translated conventionally 'Ishtar instrument') and gisŠÀ.A.TAR can be found in Akkadian lexical texts and seem to be lyres.[3] Representations of lyres are frequent on the monuments and show several types (e.g. Plates VII, VIII).[4] The Inandik vase in the Ankara Museum shows a very large lyre resting on the ground and played by two musicians, as well as five portable instruments carried in procession as on other reliefs.[5] The texts frequently distinguish a large and a small 'Ishtar instrument', so there is good correspondence between texts and monuments. Laroche has shown that the Hittite word for 'lyre' is *zinar*, *ḫunzinar* being the large variety and *ippizinar* the small one.[6] These instruments are 'struck', so this verb cannot always be taken to indicate a percussion instrument.

[1] The meaning of this phrase has now been elucidated by Kammenhuber, 1971.

[2] Other representations of the double pipes: Orthmann, 1971, 'Zincirli F/5'; Akurgal, 1962, pl. 142, from Karatepe. On the horn see Kümmel and Stauder, 1975.

[3] *Materialien zum Sumerischen Lexikon*, vi. 119.

[4] Other representations of lyres: Bossert, 1942, no. 810, from Maraş; Riemschneider, 1954, pl. 80, from Tell Halaf; Akurgal, 1962, pl. 142, from Karatepe. For Mesopotamian representations see Stauder, 1961 and 1970.

[5] See provisionally Duchesne-Guillemin, 1969, 11.

[6] Laroche, 1955b, 73.

The Sumerogram BALAG originally represented a harp (the sign is clearly recognizable in pictographic form), but it seems to have changed its meaning in the course of time and to have been used for a drum.[1] The latter sense is to be presumed for the Hittite texts, since harps are never shown on the monuments. The Hittite word for this instrument appears to be *arkammi*.[2] Both BALAG (usually BALAG.DI) and *arkammi* are constantly associated with the *galgalturi*; indeed a single singer may use both simultaneously, and they may be played by men and women while running.[3] If the *arkammi* (= BALAG.DI) is a small drum or tambourine, the *galgalturi*, which could be made of copper, but apparently also of wood,[4] could perhaps be the cymbals or clappers.[5] The only word then left for the lute, of which there are many representations (e.g. Plate VI), is *ḫuḫupal*.[6] This could be made of wood or of ivory,[7] and in one ritual it is apparently used as a drinking or libation vessel.[8] The *mukar*, which is once found as part of a chariot,[9] together with the whip, and is twice used for summoning a god into his temple,[10] could be a sistrum, such as was found at Horoztepe.[11]

The AN.TAḪ.ŠUM festival is the only one of which we have a complete outline, giving a summary of the ceremonies performed on successive days,[12] and here we find a further link with the rural rituals of the cult-inventories. On the fourteenth day in the evening a priest goes to a *tarnu* house in a grove of boxwood

[1] Hartmann, 1960, 52–5. Cf. Stauder, 1975.

[2] Both *arkammi* and BALAG.DI are frequently paired with *galgalturi*, never with each other; cf. Kümmel, 1973b, 174.

[3] In Güterbock, 1952, 32, 1–19, Ishtar picks up the BALAG.DI and the *galgalturi*, sings, and then throws them away. In *KBo* X. 24. iv. 13 (*apud* Kümmel, ibid. 175–6) the *arkammi* and the *galgalturi* are played while running (*ḫuiantes*).

[4] *KUB* X. 89. i. 27; *IBoT* I. 31 rev. 4 (among copper objects); but GIŠ-*aš-ša-an gal-gal-*[*tu-u-ri*] = 'a *galgalturi* of wood', *KUB* XII. 5. iv. 5, if the restoration is correct. However, one may also question whether the text is in order here; the sentence requires a connecting particle, such as *na!-aš-ša-an*, and 'of wood' should be GIŠ-*ru-aš*, not simply GIŠ-*aš*, e.g. *KUB* VII. 11. i. 3.

[5] Mme Danmanville, who discussed the *galgalturi* and the BALAG.DI (1962, 178–81), proposed 'tambourine' for the former but had no definite suggestion for the latter. Plates VII, VIII appear to show tambourines, to judge from the position of the hands, but the instruments in Akurgal, 1962, pl. 142, look more like cymbals. Cymbals are also apparently depicted on the Bitik vase, Özgüc, 1957, pl. IVb, and cymbals have been found at Horoztepe and elsewhere, Özgüc, 1965, 7–8. A large drum or gong is shown on Plate V. Could this also be denoted by the term BALAG?

[6] Other representations of lutes: Bossert, 1942, no. 948, from Zincirli; no. 833, from Carchemish; no. 808 (fragmentary), from Maraş, A lute of unusual shape is depicted at Alaca Hüyük: Garstang, 1929, pl. XXX; Vieyra, 1955, pl. 31; Bossert, no. 506.

[7] *KUB* XXIX. 4. i. 25.

[8] *KUB* XXV. 37. i. 34, where it is filled with wine; cf. Alp, 1940, 70 n. 2 ('ein hohles Schlaginstrument').

[9] *IBoT* I. 36. ii. 12; also with the whip, *KUB* II. 3. ii. 8.

[10] *KBo* II. 4. i. 25; *KUB* XXV. 21. iv. 6.

[11] Akurgal, 1962, pl. 12.

[12] Güterbock, 1960a; 1964, 63 ff.

trees, where there is a *ḫuwaši* stone of the Weather-god, evidently to prepare for the following day, and on the fifteenth day the king joins him there and they slaughter (*ḫuek-*) oxen and sheep at the *ḫuwaši* stone. On the nineteenth day they visit the box-wood trees again and set up cups before the Weather-god and the Sun-goddess of Arinna, and the king 'sets the race-horses on their course'. We are reminded at once of the sporting and dramatic activities already described. The ritual for the four-teenth and fifteenth days is fairly well preserved and conforms very closely to the pattern already outlined, with libations to the holy places and offerings of bread and meat before the *ḫuwaši* stone.[1] On the second day of the festival, when the king is returning to the capital from Tahurpa, there is a similar performance near a mountain called Tippuwa.[3] Here too, as we learn from the ritual for this day, there was a *ḫuwaši* stone, where the king dismounts and washes himself in a *tarnu* house. He then gets back into his chariot and drives to an 'upper *ḫuwaši* stone'. Here the men of the bodyguard race and whoever wins takes the bridle. The king alights from his chariot, breaks bread, and pours a libation in front of the *ḫuwaši* stone. He then again mounts his chariot and drives into Hattusa by 'the great road'. A footrace is also attested in the KI.LAM festival: 'ten runners come, and they give a tunic to whoever wins and who-ever comes second.'[3]

The Hittite *ḫuwaši* stone has been compared to the biblical *maṣṣēbâ* and the Hittite *ištananaš* to the biblical *ashērâ*.[4] The *maṣṣēbôṯ* and *ashērîm* are of course the two cult objects frequently mentioned as standing at the 'high places' or 'hill shrines' (*bāmôṯ*)[5] of the Canaanites and also in their temples. For example: (2 Chron. 14: 2) He suppressed the foreign altars and the *bāmôṯ*, smashed the *maṣṣēbôṯ* and hacked down the *ashērîm*;

[1] *CTH* 611.

[2] The outline tablet mentions for the second day racing at Mount Tippuwa, bathing in the *tarnu*-house and driving into Hattusa; the previous day the king and queen had been in Tahurpa. All this is described in detail in *CTH* 594, as pointed out by Güterbock (1960a, 88). *CTH* 594 is also a festival of the AN.TAḪ.ŠUM plant. It is not clear to me why it should not be the ritual for this day (it is listed by Laroche as a separate festival).

[3] *IBoT* I. 13 (*CTH* 627.11); cf. Güterbock 1964, 63 n. 49.

[4] Goetze, 1933, 158 (= 1957, 168).

[5] Vaughan, 1974, has now shown that the word *bāmâ*, which originally denoted the rib-cage or flank of an animal, was applied, at least by the Israelites to the stone-built cult platforms on which sacrifices were offered and which, though often situated on a hill-top, might equally be in a valley or inside a temple. The connection between the two essentially unrelated concepts is traced by Vaughan to the frequent allusion to God descending on to the *bāmôth* of the earth, properly the 'flanks' of the hills, but interpreted as the cult-platforms where he partook of the sacrificial offerings. The Assyriologist is reminded of the Babylonian Zigurrat.

(Deut. 12 : 3) You shall pull down their altars and break their *maṣṣēbôṯ*, burn their *ashērîm* and hack down the idols of their gods; (2 Kings 17 : 10) They built *bāmôṯ* for themselves in all their settlements . . . and set up *maṣṣēbôṯ* and *ashērîm* on every high hill and under every spreading tree; (2 Kings 10 : 26) They rushed into the keep of the temple of Baal and brought out the *ashērâ* (text: *maṣṣēbôṯ*) from the temple of Baal and burnt it, and they pulled down the *maṣṣēbâ* of Baal and the temple itself. The *maṣṣēbâ* was certainly a standing stone or stela;[1] it is translated 'pillar' or 'sacred pillar' (*NEB*). The *ashērâ* (translated 'grove' in the Authorized Version, following the Septuagint) could indeed be planted (Deut. 16 : 21) and burnt, but was also an artefact made by hand (1 Kings 16 : 33), it is thought to have been a sacred pole and a symbol of the goddess Ashera.[2] The equation of the *ashērâ* with the Hittite *ištananaš* must therefore be rejected, since the *ištananaš* was not a cult-object but a stone altar which could also be used as a support for a statue—a 'cult-stand'.[3] But the similarity of the *maṣṣēbâ* and the *ḫuwaši* stone is striking. Both are cult objects set up both in temples and in rural shrines, where they are associated with trees. Of the Hebrew and Canaanite ceremonies Robertson Smith wrote:

> The ritual observances at a Hebrew and at a Canaanite sanctuary were so similar that to the mass of the people Jehovah worship and Baal worship were not separated by any well-marked line. . . . A sacrifice was a public ceremony of a township or clan. . . . Then the crowds streamed into the sanctuary from all sides, dressed in their gayest attire, marching joyfully to the sound of music, and bearing with them not only the victims appointed for sacrifice, but store of bread and wine to set forth the feast. . . . Universal hilarity prevailed.

Each sentence here is supported by a biblical reference.[4] Like the Hittites, the Hebrews held their principle festivals in the spring and the autumn. There is even a Mishnaic tradition of racing at the autumn festival on the day of Atonement.[5]

Archaeologists are now sceptical whether most of the standing stones discovered at Palestinian sites can be properly interpreted as cult objects.[6] One has, however, recently been found at Arad,[7] and in Anatolia too one has almost certainly been found: the stela with a hieroglyphic inscription excavated in 1947 by Tahsin

[1] Barrois, 1962.
[2] Reed, 1949 and 1962.
[3] See above, p. 27. The equation with *ashērâ* appears to have been suggested by the logogram ZAG.GAR.RA = Akkad. *aširtu*; but this too is a socle or pedestal (*CAD*).
[4] Smith, 1901, 254; cf. de Vaux, 1964, 35.
[5] Yoma, ii, 1–2; Hooke, 1938, 53.
[6] Barrois, 1962.
[7] Aharoni, 1968, 19; 1969, 31.

Özgüç at Karahöyük (Elbistan), in front of which stood a trough for offerings.[1] Bossert has maintained that other known Hittite monuments were *ḫuwaši* stones, such as Restan, Apameia, Darende, Cekke, Tell Ta'iniyat, and the stela from Babylon, which must originally have been set up at Aleppo.[2] But the argument rests on some dubious etymological speculation. Only the Karahöyük stela is proved to have been a cult-object by its archaeological context.

Another feature of the AN.TAḪ.ŠUM festival must now be mentioned. On the eleventh day the chief of the palace servants 'carried the year' to the *ḫešti*-house and the king followed after him. 'He goes and sets the race-horses on their course', just as he did at the boxwood trees on the nineteenth day.[3]

The *ḫišta*- or *ḫešti*-house is commonly interpreted as a mausoleum or mortuary temple, because in a text of Hattusili III the phrase *ḫaštiyas pir* 'house of bones' appears as a variant form of the name. But the word *ḫišta* appears to be Hattic in origin and this late transformation is now considered to be an example of Hittite 'popular etymology'.[4] Rituals of the *ḫešti*-house are extant, one in Old Hittite, another a late text which is almost certainly the ritual for this eleventh day.[5] They show that it was a temple associated with a group of Hattian chthonic deities, in particular, Lelwani, the ruler of the Underworld, the fate goddesses Istustaya and Papaya, and the 'Lucky Day'.[6] What is meant by 'carrying the year' into the *ḫešti*-house? Güterbock suggested that at this spring festival the old year was ceremonially laid to rest in the 'mortuary temple' in the form of a hieroglyphic symbol.[7] But if the meaning 'mortuary temple' rests on an insecure basis, this suggestion loses its plausibility.

The *ḫešti*-house is also the place where Mursili II celebrated the *purulli* festival. He records in his Annals, at the end of his reign:

> When it became spring—whereas I had celebrated the *purulli* festival, the great festival, in honour of the Hattian Weather-god and the Weather-god of Zippalanda, but I had not celebrated the *purulli* festival, the great festival, in honour of Lelwani in the *ḫešti*-house, I therefore came up to Hattusa and celebrated the *purulli* festival, the great festival, in honour of Lelwani in the *ḫešti*-house.[8]

[1] Özgüç, 1949, pl. x; Bossert, 1952, pl. lxxiv; Darga, 1969, 16 with pls. i, ii.
[2] Bossert, 1952, 514 ff.
[3] Güterbock, 1960a, 86; 1964, 64.
[4] Kammenhuber, 1972, 300; Otten, 1975, 369.
[5] Kammenhuber, 1972, 296 ff.; *CTH* 645 and 609.
[6] See above, p. 12 with note 5.
[7] Güterbock, 1964, 67.
[8] Goetze, 1933b, 188 f.

Fragments of the ritual of this festival show that it was particularly associated with the holy city of Nerik;[1] but at this time Nerik was under enemy occupation and the Weather-god of Zippalanda took the place of the Weather-god of Nerik.[2] The Myth of Illuyanka, in which the Weather-god does battle with a dragon and after an initial defeat finally gets the better of him, is the cult myth of this festival and may well have been performed at it. A feature of this festival, at least as celebrated at Nerik, appears to have been a gathering of the gods and a blessing of the new year, recalling the ceremony which formed the climax of the new year festival at Babylon. For in the text which contains the Illuyanka myth we read that the gods of Kastama said to the priest 'When we go to the Weather-god of Nerik, where shall we dwell?'[3] And in a magical text there is the following passage:

> For the Weather-god the mighty festival of the beginning of the year, (the festival) of heaven and earth, has arrived. All the gods have gathered and come to the house of the Weather-god. If any god has sorrow in his soul, let him dispel the evil sorrow from his soul. At this festival eat and drink and be satisfied! Pronounce the life of the king and queen! Pronounce [the life] of heaven and earth, [pronounce the life] of the crops![4]

A still unpublished tablet is said to describe a similar gathering of gods for a festival of Telipinu.[5]

The AN.TAḪ.ŠUM festival and the *purulli* festival obviously have much in common. Both are celebrated in the spring by the king. The *purulli* festival is called 'the great festival' three times in successive sentences and had thirty-two tablets;[6] the AN.TAḪ.ŠUM festival is known to have lasted no less than thirty-eight days. The *purulli* festival was celebrated in the *ḫešti*-house in honour of Lelwani; this building was visited on the eleventh day of the AN.TAḪ.ŠUM festival for a ceremony called 'carrying the year'. Whether or not this means 'laying the old year to rest', it could well be the correlative of the divine assembly for blessing the new year which seems to have been part of the *purulli* festival. Were these two spring festivals in some way one and the same? It is difficult to imagine that the king could have officiated at two such lengthy festivals at the same time of year.

[1] Haas, 1970, 43 ff. [2] Ibid. 107. [3] Ibid. 46.
[4] Otten, 1956^{c}, cf. Gurney, 1958, 108. [5] Bo. 2326, quoted by Alp, 1961/2, 226.
[6] Above, p. 31 n. 7.

The Babylonian new-year festival is also relevant to the Hittite performances at the *ḫuwaši* stone. For on the eighth day, as is well known, the king 'took the hands of Marduk' and led him forth from his temple in a great procession to a building outside the city called the *akītu* house. There it is probable that the main event was a dramatic performance of the fight between Marduk and Tiamat which is the central feature of the Epic of Creation. From the *akītu* house the assembled gods returned to Babylon for the 'fixing of fates'.

Falkenstein has shown that the history of the *akītu* festival goes back to Sumerian times and that it was then celebrated, at least at Ur and Nippur, both in the spring and in the autumn.[1] Jubilation and feasting are mentioned, but there is no further information on the nature of the earlier rites. None the less, if they were in any way similar to the later ones at Babylon and Assur there is a striking parallel to the Hittite procession to the *ḫuwaši* stone. Here, as at Babylon, the god is taken out of his temple, transported to a sacred place outside the city, there is feasting and merry-making, and in some cases at least, a mock battle or a sporting event, which may be wrestling or racing, with victory for the home team. The parallel even extends to the occurrence of virtually identical festivals both in the spring and in the autumn. (The important symbolical and magical implications of the ritual combat for the prosperity of the country in the coming year need not be elaborated, since much has been written on them.)

We return now to the open-air shrine of Yazilikaya. Long ago, before the rituals had been closely studied, it was suggested that Yazilikaya with its processional road was the Hittite *akītu* house, the venue of a festival modelled on a Babylonian prototype.[2] Now that the Hittite counterpart of the *akītu* festivities is seen to be the twice-yearly procession to the *ḫuwaši* stone the question recurs in the form: 'Could Yazilikaya be the *ḫuwaši* stone of Hattusa?' The idea has been supported by reference to the text already quoted in which the king, returning from Tahurpa via Tippuwa, alights from his chariot to pour libations at two *ḫuwaši* stones, before proceeding into the city by the Great Road. Güterbock suggested tentatively in 1953 that these two spots might be identified with Yazilikaya and Büyükkaya respectively.[3] The idea was then taken up by C. W. Carter in his book on the cult inventories on the ground that 'in at least

[1] Falkenstein, 1959.
[2] References *apud* Güterbock, 1964, 72 n. 91.
[3] Güterbock, 1953, 76 n. 2.

one instance the *ḫuwaši* stone could be entered'.[1] The passage in question reads: 'The king goes in to the *ḫuwaši* stone of the Weather-god. He pays reverence to the *ḫuwaši* stone.' I do not think that 'in to' here means 'into'. The *ḫuwaši* stone of the Weather-god is elsewhere said to be in a *tarnu* house[2] and Mr. Carter himself cites a parallel passage where by the presence of the additional word *piran* it is made clear that the king goes 'in before' the *ḫuwaši* stone and pays reverence. Apart from this passage there is nothing to suggest that the term *ḫuwaši* could be applied to a major religious complex like Yazilikaya.

An alternative, for which there is more to be said, is that Yazilikaya was a *ḫešti*-house, or rather *the ḫešti*-house, since this establishment appears to have been unique.[3] The ritual of the *ḫešti*-house shows that the place had a gate-house and an inner room, and was also reached by the king in a light chariot by way of a 'great road'. Hattusili III tells us that in the bad times before Suppiluliuma I when Hattusa was sacked, the *ḫešti*-house was far enough away to escape damage. The *ḫešti*-house was originally a cult-centre for Hattian Underworld deities, but the later *ḫešti* ritual reveals that other deities of the Hattian pantheon, such as the Sun-goddess, Mezulla, Inara, Hulla, and Telipinu, were by then associated with them. In view of the completely Hurrian character of the carvings in the main chamber at Yazilikaya, the coincidence with what we know of the *ḫešti*-house is less striking than Güterbock thought when he first made this suggestion; but perhaps the *ḫešti* ritual text, late though it is, may date from before the Hurrian revolution of Queen Puduhepa and the execution of the carvings.

When we look at the smaller chamber B, the strong Underworld associations are unmistakable. The huge carving of a sword stuck into the rock and surmounted by a human head, which was for long an enigma, can now be interpreted with the aid of a passage in a magical ritual, where the group of Underworld gods known as the 'Primeval Gods' are fashioned in clay and the text reads: 'He makes them as swords and fixes them in the ground.'[4] The twelve running gods who bring up the rear of the procession in the main chamber are repeated here on the opposite wall, and it cannot be a coincidence that in another text 'the bronze swords of Nergal' and the 'twelve gods of the crossroads' are mentioned together.[5] In crevices leading out of

[1] Carter, 1962. [2] Passages cited by Darga, 1969, 13. [3] Otten, 1955, 389 ff.
[4] Otten, 1961b, 122 f., 19–20; cf. Güterbock, 1965, 198.
[5] Güterbock, 1964, 72 n. 91; 1965, 198; and *apud* Bittel, 1975, 191–2.

this chamber and in the small room 'C' behind it animal bones were found, including skeletons of birds, which appear typically in rituals connected with the Underworld.[1] All this is consistent with what we know of the *ḫešti*-house, though only in a general way.

There is, however, a third alternative. At the end of the chamber the cartouche of Tudhaliya IV is carved on the wall[2] and near it is a stone base which could once have carried his life-size statue. Further back, behind the Sword-god, this same king is shown clasped in the embracing arm of his god Sarruma (Plate II). The king and his god, like the Sword-god and the twelve running gods opposite, all face towards the statue-base and the Tudhaliya cartouche, which thus appear as the focal point of the shrine.[3] Seen in this way, the chamber can only be interpreted as a chapel in honour of the deified Tudhaliya IV. The Hittite king became a god only at his death, and though occasionally the later kings were represented on monuments with divine attributes, this is a far cry from the setting up of a chapel for the worship of a king during his lifetime. We could then identify Yazilikaya, or at least chamber B, with the *ḫekur* SAG.UŠ—literally 'permanent peak'—which is explicitly said to have been designed as a shrine in honour of Tudhaliya IV in a text of his son, Suppiluliama II.[4]

The main difficulty in this view lies in the very short time available for the three building phases II, III, and IV.[5] The small chamber was first enclosed as part of the complex in the building of Phase II. Phase III represents the addition of the free-standing propylon. In Phase IV the eastern end of the complex was completely reconstructed on a different axis, related directly to the smaller chamber. Since Suppiluliama II was the last Hittite king, we should have to suppose that this elaborate temple was built, added to, and partially reconstructed, all within the span of this single reign.

[1] Bittel, 1970, 108 f.; 1975, 53, 61 ff. For sacrifices of birds compare the following passage from the conjuration of the Underworld deities: 'He takes three birds; two birds he sacrifices to the Anunnaki, one to the god of the pit, and he speaks as follows: "Behold, you Primeval Ones! Not for you is ordained ox or sheep. When the Weather-god drove you down to the dark Underworld, he ordained this sacrifice for you"' (Otten, 1961b, 130 ff., 32–8). See Otten ad loc., and Haas and Wilhelm, 1974, 50 ff.

[2] That the cartouche, no. 83, is that of Tudhaliya IV and not that of an earlier namesake, as maintained by Beran, 1965, was proved by Otten, 1967, 226–30. It is, however, in a markedly different style from the cartouches of the same king attached to the reliefs nos. 64 and 81.

[3] Already so interpreted by Bittel, 1941, 139 ff., and Güterbock, 1953, 65.

[4] So Otten, 1963b, 22, and most recently Bittel, 1975, 256.

[5] Cf. Güterbock, 1953, 72.

A possible explanation for the partial reconstruction so soon after the first building of the temple is available in the marks of burning which show that it was destroyed by fire. The difficulty can, however, be escaped by supposing, with Otten, that the pedestal and its statue were a later addition by which Suppiluliama II transformed into a mortuary chapel an already existing shrine embellished with reliefs by Tudhaliya IV.[1] The original purpose of the chamber could then only be conjectured, but it might still be imagined that it had had some minor function in the rituals of the *ḫešti*-house which would be enacted principally in the larger chamber. In this way 'permanent peak'—a topographical term—and the functional designation *ḫešti*-house can perhaps be reconciled as names for a single establishment.[2]

[1] In the latest volume (Bittel, 1975), R. Naumann appears to have this solution in mind (pp. 123–4) when he refers to a 'Bedeutungswandel' for chamber B on the death of Tudhaliya IV: during the reign of Tudhaliya IV (Phase II) Yazilikaya would have been 'a temple with two cult-chambers'; after his death (Phase IV) there were two separate temples, with chamber B devoted to 'a special cult'. The solution implies that the reliefs 69–82, dating from the reign of Tudhaliya, are unrelated to the mortuary cult of the dead king (Otten, 1963b, 23; 1967, 240). Bittel, however, still appears to regard chamber B as a unitary design of Suppiluliama II (pp. 255–6).

[2] V. Haas and M. Wäfler (1974) have recently proposed to see in Yazilikaya a double temple to Teshub and Hebat, corresponding to Temple I in the city, and the scene of the performance of purification rites, such as the 'mouth-washing' ritual called *itkalzi*, which had to be performed outside the city to avoid contamination. The suggestion has been refuted by Güterbock (1975b), who has pointed out that Yazilikaya was as much a temple to be protected from contamination as the great temple within the city and the purification rites were performed out in the country, well away from the sacred precincts.

III

MAGICAL RITUALS

SOME years ago I wrote of the Hittite magical literature that it was not, as in Babylonia, the learned product of the temple schools, but had more the character of a national collection.[1] The contrast is striking. In Babylonia the magical texts are traditional. They take the form of instructions in the second person, the fiction being that they had been dictated by the god Ea to his son Asalluhi. The *āšipu* (or *maš-maš*) priest who carried them out had only to follow his instructions exactly. His own personality was suppressed, and he was at pains to claim divine authority for his incantations by the assertion that they were not his but those of Ea, Asalluhi, Gula, or others. He was a mere agent and his name appears only as copyist or owner of a tablet, never as author. In the scribal catalogue of authors the corpus of rituals for the *āšipu* is ascribed to the god Ea. Lambert has drawn attention to the similar practice in Egypt, where rites and spells were attributed to Thoth. Similarly, in the Old Testament the ritual instructions are communicated to Moses by God.[2]

By contrast, the Hittite magical texts are the personal prescriptions of individuals for use in particular circumstances. The name of the practitioner, with his or her profession and sometimes nationality and the nature of the emergency are stated explicitly in the opening words and in the colophon at the end of the tablet. The text purports to be the actual words of the author, sometimes in the first person, but more often in the third. Only rarely, as we shall see, is an attempt made to lend authority to the rites by attributing them to a higher power. They are simply recorded in the words of the magician and filed away for use as occasion demanded. A large proportion of the practitioners are said to be provincials from outlying parts of the kingdom, especially Kizzuwadna and Arzawa.

The typical exponent of pure 'sympathetic' magic is the so-called 'Old Woman' or 'Wise Woman'. Her profession is generally written with the Sumerogram ŠU.GI 'old', but the

[1] Gurney, 1941, 58.

[2] Lambert, 1962, 72 f. On the role of the *āšipu* in general see Ritter, 1965.

Hittite term is known to be *ḫašawaš*, a word which may be connected, or even synonymous, with *ḫašnupallaš* 'midwife'.[1] Thirteen such women are known by name,[2] but they function as sorceresses in countless rituals in which the name of the author is not preserved, and it is a reasonable assumption that the women who are attested as authors by name only can be counted among their number, which is then raised to thirty-two.[3] I know of only seven rituals whose authors are women of other professions: 3 'midwives', 1 'doctor', 1 'hierodule', 2 'temple singers'.[4]

Against this, we have some thirty-six rituals ascribed to male practitioners. The professions or these men also are usually given in the form of Sumerograms or Akkadograms, but neither *āšipu* nor *maš-maš* is found in this connection. *Āšipu* is confined to rituals written in Akkadian, with the exception of a single occurrence in the Hittite ritual of the substitute king, to which we shall return.[5] Instead, the profession of the male magician is given either simply as 'priest' or, more often, as some form of diviner. I know of thirteen rituals attributed to or performed by priests called AZU or ḪAL (Akkadian *barû*) and three further rituals attributed to *purapši*-priests, a word which appears to be the Hittite equivalent.[6] Eight such priests are known by

[1] Otten, 1952, 233 f. Kammenhuber, 1959, 70, connects with Palaic *ḫašawanza*. See now Bin-Nun, 1975, 121 ff.

[2] Annanna, Hebattarakki, Kuesa, Malli, Mallidunna, Silalluhi, Susumanniga and Tunnawiya are explicitly so called; Allaidurahi, Alli, Anniwiyani, Mastikka, and Paskuwatti are referred to as [SAL]ŠU.GI in the course of their ritual. References *apud* Laroche, 1966. For Alli see Otten, 1973b.

[3] Ayatarsa, Ambazzi, Anna, Hantitassu, Hatiya, Huntaritta, IR-mimma, Kali, Kuranna, Kururu, Nikal-uzzi, Ninalla, Belazzi, Tiwiyani, Ummaya, Uruwanda, Wattiti, Zuwi, NÍG. GA.GUŠKIN (cited by Otten, 1973b, 82), plus the thirteen named in the preceding note.

[4] Midwives: *CTH* 430 (*ḫašnupallaš*), 333 and 765 ([SAL]ŠÀ.ZU), none by name. Doctor ([SAL]A.ZU): Azzari, author of two rituals mentioned in catalogues. Hierodule ([SAL]SUḪUR. LAL): Kuwattalla, part author of *CTH* 759 and 761. Temple singers: Arsakiti (*katraš*), Kuwanni (SAL É.DINGIR-*LIM*). If *KUB* XXX. 60. i. 8 (*CTH* p. 154) is to be restored [*nu-za kar-tim*]-*mi-iš-ša* [*ši-pa-an-ti*], this could be the ritual of Kuwanni, *CTH* 474, and [SAL]*ka-at-ra-a-aš* (ibid., line 6) could be the reading of SAL É.DINGIR-*LIM*. On the other hand, the *katraš* woman was certainly a singer (Jakob-Rost, 1959), while SAL É.DINGIR-*LIM* looks more like a general term which might cover this and other professions as well.

[5] Below, p. 58. See Kümmel, 1967, 95 ff. In this text the word appears not only in its original Akkadian form but also as a Hittite loan-word [LÚ]*a-ši-pí-iš* and even with metathesis [LÚ]*a-pí-ši-iš*.

[6] AZU and ḪAL are interchangeable (Otten, 1961b, 147) and an AZU may also be called SANGA (e.g. Ammihatna in *CTH* 471 and 473.1). The following rituals are performed by men of this profession: *CTH* 400, 430, 446, 471, 473.1, 473.2 (?), 480, 483, 701, 702, 713, and two rituals mentioned in catalogues, *CTH* p. 160, 14–17, and p. 166, v. 5–7 (assuming that this and 473.2 refer to the same Ammihatna). The Ammihatna, Tulpi(ya), and Mati of *CTH* 472 (actually two rituals) are described as *purapši*-men of Kizzuwadna/Kummanni; and two *purapši*-men, [M]ati (presumably the same man) and Ammiyatalla (or Ammiyarī?), are the authors of *CTH* 473.3. If this Ammihatna and this Mati are the same individuals as Ammihatna, priest/diviner of Ishhara of Kizzuwadna, author of *CTH* 471 and 473.1, and

name from five rituals, three of which have two or three joint authors.[1] Other professions include the 'bird operator' (MUŠEN. DÙ) or augur,[2] the 'doctor' (A.ZU),[3] one *pātili*-priest,[4] one 'master of the gods',[5] and six 'priests', at least one of whom is elsewhere called a 'diviner'.[6] One ritual (*CTH* 475) is attributed to Palliya, the king of Kizzuwadna. Twenty other men are also named as authors.

Divination was a well-developed and much practised science at Hattusa, and its exponents were precisely the same three professions: the 'diviner' who was the expert in omens from the liver and entrails, the 'bird-operator' who interpreted the flight of birds,[7] and the 'Old Woman' who specialized in a type of oracle called the KIN which is little understood.[8] The records of divination do not give the names of either the 'diviners' or the 'old women'. Only the 'augurs' are occasionally mentioned by name. The 'diviner's' profession was evidently sufficient authority. Yet when the same persons practised magic, the ritual was a personal document and the practitioners were frequently foreigners. Does this mean that the priests of the college of divination indulged in magic as a part-time activity without official sanction? Certainly Hattusili I is on record as expressing strong disapproval for the activities of the 'old women'.[9]

The purposes for which magic was used were fully described and analysed by Goetze as long ago as 1933 and there is little to be added to his masterly account.[10] The methods of sympathetic magic are familiar. These simple 'analogical' methods could be employed by the Hittites in cathartic rituals almost exclusively because they treated evil for the most part as a physical contamination, not as the result of demonic malevolence.[11] Only

Mati, diviner (AZU) of Hebat (the goddess of Kummanni), author of *CTH* 702 (with Asnu-nikal and Takuya), *purapši*- could be the reading of AZU. But they could be different people and the equation is not proved.

[1] Ammihatna, Tulpi(ya), Mati, Ammiyatalla, Asnu-nikal, and Takuya (see p. 45 n. 6); Iriya, author of *CTH* 400 (= Eriya, *KUB* XXX. 50. v. 13, *CTH* p. 167), and Ehal-Teshub, author of a ritual, *KUB* XXX. 58. ii. 14 (*CTH* p. 160). 'Ammihatna' (whether one person or two) is the author of five different rituals (four mentioned in p. 45 n. 6, and *KUB* XXX. 50. v. 5–6, *CTH* p. 166).

[2] Five are named: Huwarlu, Maddunani, Dandanku, [. . . . .]-banippi and [. . . . .]-urru. See now Archi, 1975, 129 for the terms used for this profession.

[3] Hutupi (*CTH* p. 154, 20) and Zarpiya. Cf. Otten and Souček, 1969, 105 n. 15.

[4] Papanikri.

[5] Performer of *CTH* 422.

[6] Ammihatna, the diviner (see p. 45 n. 6); Ari-Teshub, Ilima-abi, Ulippi, Kantuzzili (chief priest and prince, *KUB* XXX. 56. iii. 7, *CTH* p. 181), and one unnamed, *KUB* XXX. 51. i. 7 (*CTH* p. 157).

[7] Now fully treated by Archi, 1975.

[8] Fully treated by Archi, 1974.

[9] See now Bin-Nun, 1975, 120 ff.

[10] Goetze, 1933a, 141 ff., = 1957, 151 ff.

[11] Gurney, 1941, 58; Kümmel, 1973a, 83 f.

where a god was thought to be involved was it necessary to combine them with methods proper to religion, such as prayer and sacrifice. Such composite rituals are usually performed by the male practitioners.

In this lecture I propose to deal in detail with the 'scapegoat' and other 'substitute' rituals, and secondly with the mortuary ritual for the king, which is a peculiar amalgam of magic and religion.

The Scapegoat

I have chosen the scapegoat motif because of its relevance to the well-known passage from Leviticus 16. On the Day of Atonement Aaron is instructed to take two goats and to cast lots. One goat is to be offered to the Lord for a sin offering, but the goat on which the lot falls 'for Azazel' (*RV*) is to be presented alive to make an atonement and to let it go 'for Azazel' into the wilderness. Aaron is to lay both hands on the head of the goat, confess over it all the sins of the Israelites, putting them upon the head of the goat, and to send it away into the wilderness in charge of a man who is waiting ready. 'The goat shall carry all their iniquities upon itself into some barren waste and the man shall let it go, there in the wilderness.'

The words 'for Azazel' are rendered in the Authorized Version 'for a scapegoat' and in the New English Bible (reflecting the views of Sir Godfrey Driver)[1] 'for (or to) the Precipice'. Most modern commentators, however, appear to regard Azazel as the name of a demon inhabiting the desert. T. H. Gaster has objected to this view that no known scapegoat ritual describes the animal as offered to a demon.[2] The Hittite evidence may be of some relevance here. It has, moreover, been discussed in recent years by Nadia van Brock and Hans Martin Kümmel.[3] The latter especially has presented a number of new texts and has put the whole question in a new light.

The Levitical ritual is a sublimated form of what is basically a purely magical procedure. As Frazer wrote in *The Golden Bough*:

> The notion that we can transfer our guilt and sufferings to some other being who will then bear them for us . . . arises from the very obvious confusion between the physical and the mental, between the material and the immaterial. Because it is possible to shift a load of wood, stones or what not, from our own back to the back of another, the savage

[1] Driver, 1956, 97 ff. [2] Gaster, 1962.
[3] Van Brock, 1959; Kümmel, 1967 and 1968.

fancies that it is equally possible to shift the burdens of his pains and sorrows to another who will suffer them in his stead.

In its primitive form the device is free from the ethical element of sin. What is transferred is simply 'evil', usually in fact an illness. The process of transference is effected, on the principle of 'contagious magic', simply by the physical touch of the patient, for which the priest or other officiant later acts as intermediary. In Hittite we meet this procedure at various stages of sophistication.

The first to draw attention to a Hittite scapegoat ritual was A. H. Sayce, who gave a tentative translation in the *Expository Times* in 1919.[1] As now understood, the passage runs as follows:

> If people are dying in the country, and if some enemy god has caused it, I act as follows. They drive up one ram. They twine together blue wool, red wool, green wool, black wool, and white wool, make it into a wreath and crown the ram with it. This ram they drive on to the road leading to the enemy and speak as follows: 'Whatever god of the enemy land has caused this pestilence—see! We have now driven up this crowned ram to pacify thee, O god. Just as the herd is strong and keeps peace with the ram, do thou, O god, who has caused this pestilence, keep peace with the Hatti Land.' And they drive that crowned ram towards the enemy.[2]

This is the prescription of one Uhhamuwa, a man of Arzawa. Very similar is one of the prescriptions in the ritual of Pulisa:

> If the king has been fighting the enemy and returns from the enemy country and out of the enemy country a pestilence comes and afflicts the people—they drive in a bull and a ewe—these are both from the enemy country—they decorate the bull's ears with ear-rings and (fasten on it) red wool, green wool, black wool, and white wool, and they say: 'Whatever has made the king red, green, black, or white shall go back to the enemy country.' . . . He also says: 'Whatever god of the enemy country has caused this pestilence if it be a male god, I have given thee a lusty, decorated bull with ear-rings. Be thou content with it. This bull shall take back the pestilence to the enemy country.' And he does the same with a decorated ewe if it be a female deity.[3]

Another prescription of the same kind for the same purpose, though rather more elaborate, is that of Askhella, a man of Hapalla, which is inscribed on the same tablet as the ritual of Uhhamuwa.

[1] Sayce, 1919.
[2] *CTH* 410, translated by Goetze, *ANET* 347. Miss Szabó, 1971, 98, has misread the text of line 49.
[3] *CTH* 407, translated by Kümmel, 1967, 111 ff.

When evening comes, whoever the army commanders are, each of them prepares a ram—whether it is a white ram or a black ram does not matter at all. Then I twine a cord of white wool, red wool, and green wool, and the officer twists it together, and I bring a necklace, a ring, and a chalcedony stone and I hang them on the ram's neck and horns, and at night they tie them in front of the tents and say: 'Whatever deity is prowling about(?), whatever deity has caused this pestilence, now I have tied up these rams for you, be appeased!' And in the morning I drive them out to the plain, and with each ram they take 1 jug of beer, 1 loaf, and 1 cup of milk(?). Then in front of the king's tent he makes a finely dressed woman sit and puts with her a jar of beer and 3 loaves. Then the officers lay their hands on the rams and say: 'Whatever deity has caused this pestilence, now see! These rams are standing here and they are very fat in liver, heart, and loins. Let human flesh be hateful to him, let him be appeased by these rams. And the officers point at the rams and the king points at the decorated woman, and the rams and the woman carry the loaves and the beer through the army and they chase them out to the plain. And they go running on to the enemy's frontier without coming to any place of ours, and the people say: 'Look! Whatever illness there was among men, oxen, sheep, horses, mules, and donkeys in this camp, these rams and this woman have carried it away from the camp. And the country that finds them shall take over this evil pestilence.'[1]

In these three examples the animal serves a double purpose. It carries away the infection into a foreign country, and at the same time it is offered to the hostile deity as a substitute for human flesh. The first is pure analogical magic, as described by Frazer; the infection is transferred to the animal by the laying on of hands in the Askhella ritual and by the symbolical tying of coloured wool in all three. Whether the second idea is also purely magical because—as Kümmel maintains[2]—the numen is under compulsion through the performance of the rite to accept the substitute, is questionable. At least a *prayer* is addressed to the deity, which seems to imply an element of religion. At all events, these three rituals provide a possible parallel to the dispatch of the Biblical scapegoat 'to Azazel', if this word is indeed the name of a demon.

Much simpler, but still combined with a prayer, is the ritual of Dandanku the augur:

They drive in a donkey—if it is a poor man, they make one of clay—and they turn its face to the enemy country and say: 'Thou, Yarri, hast inflicted evil on this country and its army. Let this donkey lift it and carry it into the enemy country.'[3]

[1] *CTH* 394, translated by Friedrich, 1925, 11 ff. [2] Kümmel, 1967, 4.
[3] *CTH* 425b, iii. 11–18.

Yarri, as mentioned in the first lecture, was a Luwian deity of pestilence. But this donkey is apparently nothing but a carrier and is not intended to propitiate him. Evidently, Dandanku thought it sufficient to head the animal in the right direction and pronounce the spell, if a clay donkey would do as well as a real one.

In the ritual of a woman named Ambazzi we see the magical performance in all its basic simplicity:

> She (the Old Woman) wraps up a small piece of tin in a bowstring and attaches it to the patients' right hands and feet; then she takes it off again and attaches it to a mouse, saying: 'I have taken the evil off you and attached it to this mouse. Let this mouse carry it on a long journey to the high mountains, hills and dales.'[1]

This ritual is combined with other rites in which the purpose is to appease a demon named Alawaimi, but in this particular section the magical action stands alone.

In the ritual of Huwarlu a puppy is used in a similar way:

> They take a live puppy and wave it over the king and queen, also in the palace the Old Woman waves it about, and she says: 'Whatever evil thing is in the body of the king and queen and in the palace, now see! . . . It has vanquished it. Let it carry away the evil thing and bring it to the place that the gods have appointed.' Then they take away the live puppy.[2]

From a ritual of the city of Samuha (the name of the practitioner is not preserved) we learn the technical word for such a scapegoat or animal carrier, the purpose of the ritual being to remove from the king defilement caused by curses:

> As a *nakkušši* for the king he introduces [an ox(?), and as *nakkušši*] for the queen's implements he introduces a cow, a ewe, and a goat, and while doing this he speaks as follows: 'Whatever evil oath, curse, and uncleanness have been committed before the god, these *nakkuššeš* shall carry them away from before the god. Let god and patient be cleansed from that utterance.'[3]

The fate of these animals is not described on this tablet, but the ritual probably continued on another.

[1] *CTH* 391, ii. 34–40, translated by Goetze, *ANET* 348.

[2] *CTH* 398, ii. 5 ff., translated by Kronasser, 1961/1962.

[3] *CTH* 480, rev. 58–62, translated by Goetze, *ANET* 346. Goetze assumes that this ritual is performed by the Old Woman and that she speaks the charms, but the colophon states that it is performed by Diviners ($^{\text{lú.meš}}$AZU).

Again, in a ritual of Mastikka of Kummanni occurs the following:

> Let the *nakkušši* carry off the sin, the anger, and the tears of the patient.[1]

And in the better-known ritual of this practitioner, which is directed against domestic quarrels:

> They bring in a sheep and he calls it a *nakkušši*. The Old Woman presents it to the Sun-god and says: 'O Sun-god, here is a *nakkušši* for them with mouth and tongue.' And she consecrates the sheep . . . but they do not kill it. The Old Woman takes it.[2]

Other passages about the *nakkušši* are mutilated and lack the final sentences describing its function as a carrier. They reveal, however, that not only animals and birds, but also human beings could be used as *nakkušši*. The woman used in the Askhella ritual is by no means exceptional.

The word is derived from a Hurrian root *nakk-* meaning 'let go, dispatch',[3] and must have reached the Hittites, like most Hurrian terms, from Kizzuwadna. Most of the texts quoted have connections either with Kizzuwadna or with countries further west, such as Arzawa and Hapalla. It seems that the idea of a living carrier to transport the evil away from the community was at home in Syria and the west. It does not occur in this pure form in Babylonia.[4]

That the *nakkušši* is normally a living creature follows from the nature of the concept. But in ancient times there was one inanimate vehicle which could move on its own like a living creature: a boat. And indeed there is an example in which a boat is used in exactly this way. It occurs in the ritual of Samuha, which, as already mentioned, is to remove 'evil words, oaths, and curses which have been uttered before a god'.

> They make a basin . . . and from the basin they build a small channel leading to the river. Into it they put a boat lined with a little silver and gold. They also make little oaths and curses of silver and gold and place them in the boat. Then the channel which empties the basin carries the boat from the basin into the river. When it disappears he pours out a little fine oil and honey and says: 'Just as the river has carried away the boat and no trace of it can be found any more—whoever has committed evil word, oath, curse and uncleanness in the

[1] *CTH* 405, unpublished duplicate 23/g (Kümmel, 1967, 20), cited by van Brock, 1959, 129; cf. also Rost, 1953, 377.

[2] *CTH* 404, = Rost, 1953, 361, 38–41. Translated by Goetze, *ANET* 351.

[3] Van Brock, 1959, 132 ff.

[4] Kümmel, 1967, 191–8.

presence of the god—even so let the river carry them away. And just as no trace of the boat can be found any more, let evil word not exist for my god, neither let it exist for the sacrificer's person. Let god and patient be free of that thing.'[1]

The word *nakkušši* is not applied to this boat, as it is for the animals later in the ritual, probably because the spell pronounced by the sorcerer puts it into the category of ordinary analogical magic ('just as this boat has disappeared, so may the curses disappear'). Yet the boat is used in precisely the same way as Ambazzi's mouse, even to the detail of transporting the evil in the form of small pieces of precious metal, and it must surely be regarded as originally identical in function.

The Substitute

The word *nakkušši* has commonly been translated 'substitute', but this is not strictly correct. 'Carrier' and 'substitute' are two different concepts. The Hittite word for 'substitute' is *tarpalli* or *tarpaššaš*—in which Miss van Brock proposes to see the origin of Greek θεράπων, the 'alter ego' of the Homeric heroes.[2] This is the equivalent of the Akkadian *pūḫu*, from which there is a Hurrian loan-word *puḫugari*, also used occasionally in Hittite contexts.

Strictly speaking, the magical rite for the *nakkušši* consists of transferring to it the evil or impurity which is afflicting the patient; for the substitute it lies in a symbolical act identifying the substitute with the patient. The function of the *nakkušši* is to be 'let go'; that of the *tarpalli* is to be offered in place of the patient to the numen who is thought to be attacking him. But the distinction between the two conceptions sometimes becomes blurred. In the ritual of Askhella, as we have seen, the scapegoat is treated as both a carrier and a substitute at the same time. Similarly in the Mastikka ritual, from which I have quoted a section about a sheep called a *nakkušši*, we find other animals called *tarpalleš* which are treated in both ways simultaneously:

They drive up a sheep. The Old Woman presents it to the two patients (who have quarrelled) and says: 'Here is your *tarpalli*, it shall be a *tarpalli* for your bodies. The curses are in its mouth, in its tongue.' And they spit into its mouth. Then she says: 'You have spat out the wicked curses.' Then they dig the earth and slaughter the sheep down into it. They lower it in, put down a sweet loaf for it, pour a libation, and cover it over.

[1] Cf. p. 50 n. 3. [2] Loc. cit. 126.

She takes a little dog, waves it over the two patients and says: 'This is a *tarpalli* for your whole body.' They spit into its mouth. Then she says: 'You have spat out the curses of that day.' Then they kill the little dog and bury it.[1]

From the Old Kingdom there is an example in the ritual for the royal pair, in which the king and queen spit on the substitutes and into a vessel and these are then buried.[2]

By the act of spitting, as the spell makes clear, the animal is made into a carrier, but it is not called a *nakkušši* because it is not 'let go' but is slaughtered and buried. The purpose here is to banish the evil to the Nether World and ensure that it stays there. To dig a hole in the ground is to open a communication with the Nether World. There are several Hittite rituals in which a hole is dug for the purpose of luring the infernal spirits up out of the pit. The word for such a hole is *api*, and it has been shown by Vieyra and Hoffner that the Hebrew *'ōḇ* is a cognate word, denoting not the necromancer nor the spirits and ghosts he consulted, but the hole in the ground from which they issued, thus confirming a suggestion first made by C. J. Gadd in his Schweich Lectures for 1945.[3] The present ritual uses the hole for the opposite purpose. The hole is covered over, just as it is sealed up after the spirits have returned down below, having served the purpose of the necromancer, to prevent them from returning to the earth. From mythological texts we learn that down in the Underworld there were bronze urns or bins into which all kinds of evil could be packed and sealed down with lids of lead.[4] But the buried animal with its load of curses is at the same time a substitute for the body of the client which was previously infected by them. A reference to the god Antaliya earlier in the ritual may be an indication that the animal was

[1] *CTH* 404, = Rost, 1953, 354, ii. 26–34, and 359, iii. 14–16.

[2] Otten and Souček, 1969, see index s.v. *allapaḫ-* and *ḫarii̯a-*. Many points in this early text remain obscure. Cf. Haas and Wilhelm, 1974, 47–8.

[3] Gadd, 1948, 89; Vieyra, 1957, 100; 1961, 47–55; Hoffner, 1967a.

[4] This 'mythologeme' occurs in the Telipinu myth, *CTH* 324, 1st version (*RHA* 77, 97, 15–17) and 2nd version (ibid. 103 f., 7–9), in the myth of the disappearance of the Weather-god, *CTH* 325 (ibid. 118, 6–8), in the myth of the Weather-god at Lihzina, *CTH* 331 (ibid. 130, 9 ff.), and in the myth of the disappearance of ᵈMAḪ, *CTH* 334 (ibid. 139, 5–7). In most of these passages the *palḫi* vessels are down in the Underworld, but in *CTH* 331 they are in the sea, while in the magical ritual of Hutusi, *CTH* 732, a similar vessel stands on or by a pyre and is similarly used for disposing of rubbish. A cup (*zeri*) with a leaden lid serves the same purpose in Otten and Souček, 1969, 38. iv. 35. Hoffner, 1968a, 65 f., compares Zech. 5: 7–8, where a figure representing wickedness is confined in a container with a leaden lid. I do not know of any evidence that these *palḫi* vessels were 'cauldrons', i.e. vessels for boiling liquids. In the Illuyanka Myth they are vats containing beer and wine. Cf. *ANET* 128; Otten, 1958a, 141; Otten and von Soden, 1968, 30; Vieyra, 1965, 129; Hoffner, 1973, 217–18 and 227 n. 12.

regarded as an offering to him, though he is not the cause of the trouble.[1]

The substitute may be identified verbally with the patient, part by part.[2] This is a practice well attested in the Babylonian magical texts, and it is found in Hittite mainly in rituals of Luwian origin which may have come to Hattusa via Kizzuwadna, but ultimately from Mesopotamia. The body parts are conventionally counted as twelve, but the number actually enumerated is erratic. Thus it is said of a sheep:

> Its head represents his head. Its forehead represents his forehead. Its nose represents his nose. Its mouth represents his mouth. Its throat represents his throat. Its lung represents his lung. Its genitals represent his genitals.[3]

A similar passage for a ram, enumerating eighteen bodily parts, ends as follows:

> His twelve bodily parts I have prepared. Now see, the bodily parts of the ram shall summon forth the sickness of the man's parts.[4]

Another passage, in which the substitute is probably an effigy, enumerates the figure, the head, the nose, the eyes, the ears, the mouth, the tongue, the throat, the neck, the back, the arm, the chest, the heart, the liver, the lung, the shoulder, the genitals, the stomach, the penis, the thighs, the knees, and the toes—twenty-two parts in all.[5]

It is characteristic of these Luwian texts that divine authority is claimed for the ritual by a piece of mythology attributing it to the goddess Kamrusepa. In one such text the purification is effected by combing:

> The Sun-god and Kamrusepa are combing sheep. They are vying with each other and wrangling. Then Kamrusepa placed an iron chair and put on it a wool-comb of lead. They combed a pure kid. They scrubbed(?) it and washed it. . . . They had it for the purpose of treating the man. They are treating the twelve bodily parts of the man.[6]

In the myth of the missing god, Telipinu, the same goddess makes use of sheep from the herd of the Sun-god to charm away the anger of the god. The use of this 'mythologeme' here gives the text a Luwian colouring.

More commonly the substitute is identified with the patient simply by waving it over him, as in the Mastikka ritual. If it is

[1] Rost, 1953, 351, i. 34, with note p. 371.
[2] Haas, 1971, *passim*.
[3] *KBo.* VIII. 73; Haas, 1971, 423.
[4] *KUB* IX. 34. ii. 35–7.
[5] *KUB* XLIII. 53. i. 1 ff.
[6] *KUB* XII. 26. ii. 1–10; Haas, 1971, 423–4.

an effigy or another human being, it may be dressed up in his clothes. Once it is a 'pot', which Kümmel suggests may have been a 'face vase'.[1]

The function of the substitute is—as S. H. Hooke put it—to act as a lightning conductor by diverting the divine wrath away from the threatened victim.[2] If the patient is sick, there is a potential threat of death, and if no other deity is known to be the cause, the substitute is offered to the Queen of the Underworld, in accordance with the belief first attested in the Sumerian myth of the Descent of Inanna, that a victim once claimed by the Underworld can only be rescued by the provision of a substitute.[3] The wife of Mursili II, Gassuliyawiya, suffered from a mortal illness, and we have a prayer in which she tells how she dispatched a woman as *tarpalli* to Lelwani (here the old Hattian god, not a goddess):

> If thou, O god, my lord, art seeking ill of me . . ., this (woman) (shall be) my substitute (*tarpašša-*). I am presenting her to thee in fine attire. Compared to me she is excellent, she is pure, she is brilliant, she is white, she is decked out with everything. Now, O god, my lord, look well on her. Let this woman stand before the god, my lord.[4]

The actual fate of this female substitute is unfortunately lost in a lacuna. Later in the text other substitutes prepared by Gassuliyawiya, presumably effigies, are apparently burned.

Mursili II himself provides another example. In a text resembling a royal edict the king tells us that he suffered from some form of aphasia, apparently brought on by a thunderstorm.[5] When the trouble persisted, he consulted the diviners and was informed—not surprisingly—that it was due to the anger of the Weather-god. The prescribed cure was the dispatch of a substitute-ox to the temple of the Weather-god at Kummanni, accompanied by a ritual couched in the typical Hurrian terminology of Kizzuwadna. Here the term used for the substitute is the Hurrian word *puḫugari*. On arrival at the temple the animal is to be presented to the god and burned, together with some birds. If it should happen to die on the long journey, another animal must be substituted and burned in its place. An ox was duly selected and decorated, identified with the king by the laying on of his hands, and dispatched to Kummanni. The text does not reveal whether the king was cured.

[1] Rost, 1953, 364, iv. 9 ff.; cf. Kümmel, 1967, 21 n. 69.
[2] Hooke, 1952, 4.
[3] Kramer, 1969, 116–17.
[4] *CTH* 380, obv. 10 ff. (Kümmel, 1967, 120 f.). Cf. Otten, 1950, 128.
[5] Goetze, 1934.

We may note in passing the practice of burning the substitute —at least the substitute for the king and queen. The same practice is found in another ritual, unfortunately fragmentary.[1] The text just quoted appears to specify this as a method of offering to the god, not merely as an effective form of destruction. The sacrifice of birds, as already remarked, is associated with the Underworld.[2] But why are they burned? Kümmel has raised the interesting question whether there is a connection with the West Semitic burnt offering or holocaust, Hebrew *'ôlāh*, which cannot be ruled out.[3]

The most notable example of the use of the *tarpalli* substitute is in the ritual of the substitute king, of which we now have two versions edited by Dr. Kümmel. Here the threat of death arises from an omen or an oracle.

The beginning of the first text is lost. It sets in at a point where the king is praying to the Moon-god:

'Now, in the matter about which I have come before thee, hear me, O Moon-god, my lord. Since thou, Moon-god, hast given me a sign, lest thou wert signalling evil thereby, see! I have appointed substitutes (*tarpalliuš*) in my place. Now take these (but let me go free).' Then they drive a live bull up on to the high place of the Moon-god and they consecrate it up there on the high place.

The following lines are mutilated, but it is clear that the bull is killed and (once again) burnt, allegedly because the Moon-god had wished to see (not smell!) the smoke of the king's funeral.[4] The king prays: 'Let these substitutes die, but I will not die.' When the text sets in again, there is reference to an effigy and then a prisoner of war is introduced:

They anoint the prisoner with the fine oil of kingship, and the king says: 'See, this is the king. I have given him the name of kingship, have clothed him in the garment of kingship, have set the crown on his head. Now, evil omen, short years, short days, recognize him! Go after this substitute!' Then he departs to the city. . . . Then they bring an officer to the prisoner and he takes him back to his own country.

[1] *KUB* VII. 10 (Kümmel, 1967, 129 ff.).

[2] See above, p. 42 n. 1.

[3] Kümmel, 1967, 23 f. Kümmel considers only the *'ôlâ*, but it may be noted that the *iššeh*, the portion of the communion sacrifice offered to Yahweh 'for a sweet savour', is also regularly burned (e.g. Lev. 3: 5). In the ritual of Zarpiya quoted above (p. 30) the god's portion is cooked (roasted?) with fire.

[4] In a parallel text (Kümmel, p. 37) a substitute bull is clearly burned and the smoke is seen by the Sun-god of Heaven.

This passage has long been known as the only evidence we have for the procedure at a king's coronation.[1] It happens also to be the only text where the final fate of the substitute king is preserved, and here he is rather unexpectedly dispatched abroad like a *nakkušši*.

The text continues with a ritual of sacrifice. The king offers sheep to the Sun-god (probably the 'Sun-goddess of Earth' is intended[2]—the text seems to be in disorder here),[3] the Moon-god and Lelwani, each time praying that the god will accept the *tarpalli* and let him go free. In each of these prayers there is a reference to the infernal deities, in whose power he has been placed by the evil omen. The end of the text is again lost.

The second ritual has a well-preserved colophon stating its purpose:

> If death is predicted for the king, whether he sees it in a dream or it is made known to him by divination from the entrails or by augury, or if some omen of death occurs in front of him, this is the ritual for it.

The beginning is again missing, but we have the last few words of the robing of the prisoner of war. The text then continues:

> Then they construct in a separate place a hut and in it a wooden effigy with eyes of gold and ear-rings of gold. They dress it in royal robes and a spare set of robes is laid aside for it [there follows a list of garments, etc.]. They set up 2 tables, right and left, and 7 loaves on the table, right and left. They set 7 loaves twice daily for it and daily they sacrifice a sheep for it; the king eats some (of it) daily and they bring food daily to the effigy. But when they bring it, no one sees it; they cover it over and so place it before the effigy.
>
> Then the king says: 'This is the living supernal substitute for me, and this effigy is the infernal substitute for me. If you, heavenly gods, have afflicted me with evil or shortened my days, months, or years, this living substitute man shall stand in my place; mark him well, O heavenly gods. But if the Sun-goddess of the Underworld and the infernal gods have afflicted me, then this effigy shall stand in my place; mark it well, O infernal gods.' The king sits down.
>
> Then they bring the prisoner in. . . . He says to the king: 'Leave the palace!' The king answers: 'I will go.' . . . When he has uttered these words, he goes down from the palace and no one speaks his name any more. . . . If anyone comes up into the city, people do not say 'The city

[1] Goetze, 1933, 84 n. 2; Vieyra, 1939, 126 ff.; Gurney, 1958, 118. Kümmel has a full discussion of the evidence for the Hittite coronation ceremony (pp. 43–9).

[2] On this title see above, p. 5, and Laroche, 1974.

[3] Kümmel, p. 34.

in which the real king is'—not so (but) 'The city in which the new king is, that is where the king is.' And the king kneels daily before the Sun-god of heaven in the early morning and prays: 'Sun-god of heaven, my lord, what have I done? Thou hast taken the throne away from me and given it to another. . . . Thou hast summoned me to the shades. But I have appeared before thee, Sun-god of heaven. Release me from the realm of the shades.'

Then they perform the royal ritual for the new king. They serve him with food and drink, his bed is placed in the bedroom, the chamberlains watch over him at night, . . . he sits down in the place where the true king sits. But on the seventh day—

and here the single sign that is preserved can hardly be anything but the beginning of the word for 'he dies'.[1] The rest of this text is badly mutilated, and we do not learn what happens to the effigy, the 'infernal substitute'. But even the 'supernal substitute' is apparently put to death. That the prisoner in the first ritual is merely sent away to his own country is surely out of line with the role of the *tarpalli* and looks like a case of contamination with the *nakkušši* ritual. There is a similar confusion in the ritual of Pulisa where a prisoner of war is treated in just this way but is called *PUḪIŠU* 'substitute',[2] although the ritual is concerned, not with the king, but with an epidemic among the people, and is followed immediately by the *nakkušši* ritual quoted earlier.

It need hardly be said that the Hittite rituals of the substitute king are closely parallel to what is known of this custom in Mesopotamia. There too the installation of a substitute king was normally for the purpose of averting an evil omen. As W. G. Lambert writes: 'It is clear that when an eclipse occurred which, according to the omen texts, should have resulted in the king's death, a substitute was temporarily put on the throne to die in place of the real monarch, who was thus saved.'[3] This is exactly what we find in the Hittite texts. They provide, moreover, welcome amplification of our knowledge of the ritual which is only preserved as a mutilated fragment in the Babylonian literature. Indeed the occurrence in these texts of many Akkadian terms which occur nowhere else in Hittite, such as *āšipu* for the exorcist, gives rise to the suspicion that they go back ultimately to Babylonian originals.

1 Kümmel, pp. 93–4, restores *a*-[*ki*].

2 Ibid., pp. 111 ff., with commentary p. 81 on the peculiar use of *PU-UḪ-ŠU*, *PU-ḪI-ŠU*, pl. *PU-UḪ-ŠU*ḪI.A., *PU-UḪ-ŠI*ḪI.A, in place of the simple *PŪḪU*.

3 Lambert, 1957b, 109.

Funerary Ritual

We turn now from the magical rituals of substitution designed to preserve the life of the king to the elaborate funerary rites which were performed when he actually died. Here again, not unnaturally, the Nether World and the chthonic powers are constantly in mind and effigies or 'infernal substitutes' play a prominent part. This fourteen-day ritual has been partly reconstructed by H. Otten out of many fragments, but unfortunately there are still large gaps and many details are scarcely intelligible.[1] It is placed by Laroche in his *Catalogue* in the category of magical rituals, and indeed the Old Woman and her magical practices constantly recur throughout it. These practices, however, are here combined with rites typical of the temple cult, such as 'drinking to' various gods and to the soul of the deceased, and many passages describing the performance of the musicians are indistinguishable from passages in the festival rituals.

The main ritual, to which most of the fragments appear to belong, is entitled 'If in Hattusa a great calamity happens, (namely) either the king or the queen becomes a god'. The word here translated 'calamity' is *wastaiš*, normally 'sin', which obviously has overtones difficult to indicate in an English rendering. The death of the king or queen seems to have been regarded as a violation of the divine order of things. As is now well known, these texts, and the concurrent discovery of urns buried among the rocks at Osmankaya near the capital,[2] revealed that Hittite kings were cremated. The actual cremation is unfortunately not preserved, but it must have taken place during the second night. There is a fragment from the very beginning of the ritual: they slaughter an ox at the dead man's head and pronounce the words 'Let down your soul into this ox'. A libation is poured to the soul, and a goat is waved over the body. Presumably the ox and the goat are regarded as substitutes, either to be buried and sealed down, like Mastikka's animals, or perhaps to be burned, but the text breaks off and the continuation is mutilated. Night falls, and the rites for the following day include the offering of food and drink to the dead. It seems that this is counted as the first day.

When the second day dawns, the cremation is already completed. At first light women come and quench the fire and collect

[1] Otten, 1958a, 1958b, and 1962; Laroche, 1961; Christmann-Franck, 1971; *CTH* 450.
[2] Bittel, 1958.

the bones in a silver vessel (*lappa-*)—note the frequent use of silver as the metal of purity.[1] They soak them in oil, wrap them in linen cloths and place them on a chair (if it be a man) or a stool (if a woman). A table is set, the women eat and drink to the soul of the dead. Now a human figure is made out of figs, raisins, and olives, placed on the pyre and filled with food and drink, apparently for the purpose of attracting the spirit of the dead into it.

There follows a strange piece of dialogue between two 'Old Women' involving the symbolic use of a balance:

> The Old Woman takes a balance. Into one scale she puts gold, silver, and all kinds of precious stones. Into the other she puts mortar (mud). The Old Woman says to her companion—indicating the deceased by name: 'Who is going to "bring" So-and-so?' And her companion answers: 'The Hittites, the *uruḫḫa*-men, will "bring" him.' But the first one says: 'They shall not "bring" him.' Her companion answers: 'Take the silver and the gold!' But she says: 'I will not take it.' She says this three times. And at the third time the first one(?) says: 'I will take the mortar.'[2] Then she breaks the balance and [lays(?)] it in front of the Sun-god. . . .

It seems that the balance is not, as in ancient Egypt, the symbol of rectitude but rather the instrument typifying a market transaction. The silver, gold, and precious stones are the price; the mud presumably represents the deceased person. The closest parallel is a passage, unfortunately badly damaged, from a ritual of exorcism, where the words specifying the contents of the second scale are lost:[3]

> She pours silver, gold, and precious stones . . . on a balance and opposite to [. . . .] they weigh six times, and they speak as follows: 'Sun-god [of blood] and Weather-god, behold! The master, with his wife and children [is weighed(?)] for you. Be appeased!'

This, surely, can only mean that the price is paid, the sinners are redeemed.[4] In the funerary ritual something similar is to be expected. Perhaps the dead person is imagined as being offered for sale to the *uruḫḫa*-men (whoever they may be); but their price is refused, he is redeemed.

[1] Cf. Haas and Wilhelm, 1974, 38 f.

[2] Reading *šal-u-i-na-an-wa-za* (Otten, 1962, 231), a correction missed by Miss Christmann-Franck in her translation.

[3] Szabó, 1971, 26, 41–4.

[4] Miss Szabó translates '(auf)gewogen', and on p. 101 she says the precious metals and stones are weighed as a sign of the innocence of the sacrificer. This suggests that she was thinking of the gold and silver as symbolic of purity. If so, there would be a closer resemblance to the Egyptian weighing of the soul against the symbol of truth than I believe to be the case. The verb *ušneškimi* 'I am selling' in 406/c (*KBo* XXI. 22), quoted by Otten, 1958a, 132, points clearly in the direction of a mundane symbol of the market.

After this there is a lacuna. Then, after sacrifices to the Sun-goddess of the Underworld and the soul of the dead, the bones are brought to the 'stone house' or mausoleum and placed on a bed; a lamp is lit. Here on the third day there is a ceremony with sacrifices and drinking to Mezulla and other gods, accompanied by music. The following days are lost, but on the seventh we find there is an effigy seated on a chariot, which the women take out of the house to the courtyard. Here *ezzan* (possibly here the dead man's personal property)[1] is burned, together with a fine garment and a jar of oil. Another cult meal takes place together with drinking and music. On the eighth day oxen, sheep, horses, and mules are slaughtered for the deceased; the Old Woman declares that they are his property and no one shall take them away from him. A 'piece of meadow' is also brought and she declares that the animals shall graze on it. After the seated effigy has again been toasted, it is taken off the chariot into a tent and placed on a golden throne (or, in the case of a woman, on a stool). Another feast takes place with drinking and music. In the evening of this day there is a mutilated reference to another figure made of fruit, or in the case of a woman, of cereals. The ninth day is almost entirely lost. On the tenth day a plough is burned and the ashes are brought to the place where 'the heads of the horses and cattle were burned', which implies that this holocaust had taken place at the time of the cremation. The eleventh day is again missing, but the twelfth is well preserved. The day opens with the effigy in the house. There are sacrifices to it and to the chthonic powers, to the ancestors and to the soul of the dead. The effigy is then put on a chariot and taken out, followed by mourning women. A vine is cut, decked out with natural and artificial grapes and other things, and taken into a tent. Here the effigy is brought and there is another meal with music. After this a kinsman of the dead cuts down the vine with a silver axe, the effigy is put back on the chariot and taken back, perhaps to the house. The thirteenth day begins with an obscure performance with models of birds. They are apparently pushed in at the window and then burned.[2] There is another cult meal with music. Then the effigy with the throne is placed on a platform and further sacrifices of oxen and sheep take place. This is repeated nine times and followed again by further drinking to the 'Lucky

[1] Following Goetze, 1960, 378, as neither salt not chaff (Laroche, 1961) make very good sense here.

[2] On the burning of birds and the connection of birds with the Underworld see above, p. 56.

Day', the Sun-goddess of the Underworld, and the ancestors. Finally, bread is laid on the effigy's knees and they say: 'See, we have placed the bread on your legs. Now don't be angry any more! Be kind to your children! Your kingdom shall endure for your grandchildren and great-grandchildren.' They then bring a rope, smear it with oil, throw it on the hearth and say: 'When you go to the meadow, do not pull the rope!' The day ends with more offerings and the removal of the tent to the entrance. The fourteenth day is not preserved and so the end of the ritual is unknown, but there can be little doubt that the remains of the dead were finally laid to rest in the Stone House.

To judge from the final address, the Hittites, like other ancient peoples, were acutely aware of the potential menace posed by the soul of the dead, and especially of a royal personage, and the whole elaborate rite was primarily devised for its propitiation. It must not only be offered food and drink in plenty but must also be provided with a suitably affluent life-style in the Elysian fields. For it is clear that something of this kind was envisaged for the king in the afterlife.[1] He was provided symbolically with a meadow and with cattle to graze on it. Presumably the plough which is burned on the eighth day is connected with the same idea, but the significance of the rope which must not be pulled is obscure.

The ritual clearly establishes that the bones of the king were laid to rest in a building called a 'Stone House'. Stone Houses of Suppiluliuma, Arnuwanda, and Tudhaliya are attested. They were considerable establishments, endowed with lands and villages and a personnel which included herdsmen, peasants, house servants, and gatekeepers. These people and their families were attached to the establishment for life and forbidden to leave it even for marriage. They were, however, exempt from taxes and public service and an *eyan* tree—apparently an ever-green—was planted in front of the Stone House as a symbol of this freedom.[2]

We conclude by referring, for the third and last time, to Yazilikaya. We have suggested that this intriguing holy place was the *ḫesti* house where the New Year festival called *purulli* was celebrated and where the old year appears to have been laid to rest on the eleventh day of the spring festival of AN. TAḪ.ŠUM. We have shown good reason for thinking that the

[1] Otten, 1958a, 139; Vieyra, 1965, 127 ff.

[2] *CTH* 252; Otten, 1958a, 104 ff., 132 f. The erection of an *eyan* tree as a symbol of exemption from imposts is attested in the Laws, § 50.

small chamber was laid out as a mortuary chapel for Tudhaliya IV. Was it also his Stone House? It has always been evident that *ḫesti* house and Stone House had much in common. One eminent scholar has now expressed the opinion that they are synonymous terms,[1] and it was long ago suggested that the three large cavities or niches at the back of the chamber might have been ossuaries or repositories for the urns containing the ashes of the dead king. However, the cavities were found empty and intensive excavation has failed to produce any clear evidence of a burial. The possibility that in Yazilikaya Chamber B we have the Stone House of Tudhaliya IV will probably for ever remain no more than an attractive hypothesis.

[1] Kammenhuber, 1972, 300.

BIBLIOGRAPHY

AHARONI, Y., 1968. 'Arad, its inscriptions and temple', in *The Biblical Archaeologist*, 31, 2–31.

—— 1969. 'The Israelite sanctuary at Arad', in *New Directions in Biblical Archaeology*, ed. D. N. Freedman and J. C. Greenfield (New York).

AKURGAL, E., 1962. *The Art of the Hittites*. London.

ALP, S., 1940. *Untersuchungen zu den Beamtennamen im hethitischen Festzeremoniell* (Sammlung orientalistischer Arbeiten 5). Leipzig.

—— 1947. 'La désignation du Lituus en hittite', in *JCS* 1, 164–75.

—— 1961/2. 'Eine hethitische Bronzestatuette und andere Funde aus Zara bei Amasya', in *Anatolia*, 6, 217–43.

ARCHI, A., 1966. 'Trono regale e trono divinizzato nell'Anatolia ittita', in *SMEA* 1, 76–120.

—— 1974. 'Il sistema KIN della divinazione ittita', in *Oriens Antiquus*, 13, 113–44.

—— 1975. 'L'ornitomanzia ittita', in *SMEA* 16, 119–80.

ASTOUR, M. C., 1968. 'Semitic elements in the Kumarbi myth', in *JNES* 27, 172–7.

BALTZER, K., 1960. *Das Bundesformular*. Neukirchen.

BARNETT, R. D., 1953. 'The Phrygian rock façades and the Hittite monuments', in *BiOr* 10, 78–82.

—— 1956. 'Ancient oriental influences in archaic Greece', in *The Aegean and the Near East, Studies Presented to Hetty Goldman* (ed. S. S. Weinberg) (New York).

BARROIS, G. A., 1962. 'Pillar', in *Interpreter's Dictionary of the Bible*, K–Q, 815–17.

BERAN, T., 1965. 'Zum Datum der Felsreliefs von Yazilikaya', in *ZA* 57, 258–73.

—— 1967. *Die hethitische Glyptik von Boğazköy* (*WVDOG* 76). Berlin.

BIN-NUN, S. R., 1975. *The Tawannanna in the Hittite Kingdom* (Texte der Hethiter 5). Heidelberg.

BITTEL, K., 1934. *Die Felsbilder von Yazilikaya* (Istanbuler Forschungen 5). Bamberg.

—— 1941. *Yazilikaya* (*WVDOG* 61). Leipzig.

—— 1952. *Boğazköy-Hattuša. I. Architektur, Topographie, Landeskunde und Siedlungsgeschichte* (*WVDOG* 63). Stuttgart.

—— 1958. *Boğazköy-Hattuša. II. Die hethitischen Grabfunde von Osmankayasi* (*WVDOG* 71). Berlin.

—— 1964. 'Einige Kapitel zur hethitischen Archäologie', in *Neuere Hethiterforschung*, ed. G. Walser (*Historia*, Einzelschriften 7).

—— 1970. *Hattusha, the Capital of the Hittites*. New York.

—— 1975. *Boğazköy-Hattuša. IX. Das hethitische Felsheiligtum Yazilikaya*. Berlin.

Bossert, H. T., 1942. *Altanatolien*. Berlin.

—— 1952. 'Das H-H Wort für "Malstein" ', in *Belleten*, XVI/64, 495–545.

—— 1955. 'Die hieroglyphenhethitische Inschrift von Kötükale', in *Le Muséon*, 68, 61–91.

—— 1957. 'Die Schicksalsgöttinnen der Hethiter', in *Die Welt des Orients*, 2, 349–59.

Brandenstein, C.-G., 1943. 'Hethitische Götter nach Bildbeschreibungen in Keilschrifttexten', in *MVAG* 46 (2).

van Brock, N., 1959. 'Substitution rituelle', in *RHA* XVII/65, 117–46.

Burde, C., 1974. *Hethitische medizinische Texte* (*StBoT* 19). Wiesbaden.

Carruba, O., 1966. *Das Beschwörungsritual für die Göttin Wisurijanza* (*StBoT* 2).

—— 1968. 'Anatolico *Runda*', in *SMEA* 5, 31–41.

—— 1969. 'Die Chronologie der hethitischen Texte und die hethitische Geschichte der Grossreichszeit', in *ZDMG* Suppl. I, 226–49.

—— 1970. *Das Paläische. Texte, Grammatik, Lexikon* (*StBoT* 10). (Wiesbaden.)

Carter, C. W., 1962. *Hittite Cult Inventories*. (Dissertation, Chicago.)

Christmann-Franck, L., 1971. 'Le rituel des funérailles royales hittites', in *RHA* XXIX, 61–111.

Danmanville, J., 1962. 'Iconographie d'Ištar-Šaušga en Anatolie ancienne', in *Revue d'assyriologie*, 56, 9–30, 113–31, 175–90.

—— 1975. 'Hepat, Hebat', in *RlA* IV, 326–9.

Darga, M., 1969. 'Über das Wesen des *ḫuwaši*-Steines nach hethitischen Kultinventaren', in *RHA* XXVII/84–5, 5–20.

Delaporte, L., 1936. *Les Hittites*. Paris.

Dinçol, A. M., and Darga, M., 1969/70. 'Die Feste von Karaḫna', in *Anatolica*, 3, 99–118.

Driver, G. R., 1956. 'Three technical terms in the Pentateuch', in *Journal of Semitic Studies*, 1, 97–105.

Duchesne-Guillemin, M., 1969. 'La théorie babylonienne des métaboles musicales', in *Revue de musicologie*, 55, 3–11.

Dussaud, R., 1945. 'Les religions des Hittites et des Hourrites, des Phéniciens et des Syriens', in *Mana*, *Les Anciennes Religions orientales*, II, 333–414. Paris.

Ehelolf, H., 1925. 'Wettlauf und szenisches Spiel im hethitischen Ritual', in *SPAW* 1925, 267–72.

Falkenstein, A., 1959. '*akiti*-Fest und *akiti*-Festhaus', in *Festschrift Johannes Friedrich*, 147–82.

Forrer, E. O., 1936. 'Eine Geschichte des Götterkönigtums aus dem Hethiterreiche', in *Mélanges Franz Cumont* (*Annuaire de l'Institut de Philologie et d'Histoire orientales et slaves* IV), 687–713. Brussels.

—— 1938. 'Quelle und Brunnen in Alt-Vorderasien', in *Glotta*, 26, 178–202.

Frantz-Szabó, G., 1975. 'Ḫuwaššanna', in *RlA* IV, 528–9.

Friedrich, J., 1924. 'Der hethitische Soldateneid', in *ZA* 35, 161–92.

—— 1925. 'Aus dem hethitischen Schrifttum, 2. Heft', in *Der Alte Orient*, 25 (2).

FRIEDRICH, J., 1926/1930. 'Staatsverträge des Hatti-Reiches in hethitischer Sprache', I, in *MVAG* 31.1 (1926), II, in *MVAG* 34.1 (1930).

—— 1952. 'Zu einigen altkleinasiatischen Gottheiten', in *JKF* 2, 145–53.

—— 1957. 'Ein hethitisches Gebet an die Sonnengottheit der Erde', in *Rivista degli studi orientali*, 32, 217–24.

FURLANI, G., 1934. 'Mursilis II e il concetto del peccato presso gli Hittiti', in *Studi e Materiali di Storia delle Religioni*, 10, 19–37.

—— 1935. 'Il giudizio del dio nella dottrina religiosa degli Hittiti', in *RHA* III/18, 30–44.

—— 1936. *La Religione degli Hittiti*. Bologna.

—— 1938. 'The basic aspect of Hittite religion', in *Harvard Theological Review*, 31, 251–62.

GADD, C. J., 1948. *Ideas of Divine Rule in the Ancient Near East*. (The Schweich Lectures, 1945.) London.

GARSTANG, J., 1914. 'The Sun-God[dess] of Arenna', in *Annals of Archaeology and Anthropology* (Liverpool), VI, 109–15.

—— 1929. *The Hittite Empire*. London.

GASTER, T., 1962. 'Azazel', in *Interpreter's Dictionary of the Bible*, A–D, 325–6.

GOETZE, A., 1930. 'Die Pestgebete des Muršiliš', in *Kleinasiatische Forschungen*, 1, 161–251.

—— 1933a. *Kleinasien*. (I. von Müller, *Handbuch der Altertumswissenschaft* III. 1. iii). 2nd edn., 1957.

—— 1933b. 'Die Annalen des Muršiliš', in *MVAG* 38.

—— 1934 (with H. PEDERSEN). *Muršilis Sprachlähmung*. (*Det Kgl. Danske Videnskabernes Selskab, hist.-filol. Meddelelser* XXI. 1). Copenhagen.

—— 1938. *The Hittite Ritual of Tunnawi* (American Oriental Series 14). New Haven.

—— 1940. 'The Ugaritic deities *pdgl* and *ibnkl*', in *Orientalia*, 9, 223–9.

—— 1953. 'The theophorous elements of the Anatolian proper names from Cappadocia', in *Language*, 29, 263–77.

—— 1954a. 'Some groups of ancient Anatolian proper names', in *Language*, 30, 349–59.

—— 1954b. 'The linguistic continuity of Anatolia', in *JCS* 8, 74–81.

—— 1957. See 1933 (2nd edn.).

—— 1960. Review of Otten, *Hethitische Totenrituale*, in *American Journal of Archaeology*, 64, 377–8.

—— 1962. Review of *KBo* X (*WVDOG* 72), in *JCS* 16, 24–30.

—— 1963. Review of *KBo* XII (*WVDOG* 77), XIV (*WVDOG* 79) and *KUB* XXXIX, in *JCS* 18, 89–96.

—— 1970/1. 'Hittite *šipant-*', in *JCS* 23, 76–94.

GONNET, H., 1968. 'Les montagnes d'Asie Mineure d'après les textes hittites', in *RHA* XXVI/83, 93–171.

GORDON, E. I., 1967. 'The meaning of the ideogram ^{d}KASKAL.KUR = "underground watercourse"', in *JCS* 21, 70–88.

GÜTERBOCK, H. G., 1946. *Kumarbi.* (Istanbuler Schriften 16.) Zürich, New York.

—— 1947. 'Ein hethitisches Relief aus der Umgebung von Boğazköy', in *Belleten*, XI/42, 189–95.

—— 1949. 'Hittite Religion', in *Forgotten Religions*, ed. Vergilius Ferm (Philosophical Library, New York).

—— 1952. *The Song of Ullikummi. Revised Text of the Hittite Version of a Hurrian Myth.* New Haven. (Reprinted from *JCS* 5–6.)

—— 1953. 'Yazilikaya', in 'Vorläufiger Bericht über die Ausgrabungen in Boğazköy im Jahre 1952', *MDOG* 86, 65–76.

—— 1959. 'Gedanken über das Wesen des Gottes Telipinu', in *Festschrift Johannes Friedrich*, 207–11.

—— 1960a. 'Outline of the Hittite AN.TAḪ.ŠUM festival', in *JNES* 19, 80–9.

—— 1960b. 'Mursili's accounts of Suppiluliuma's dealings with Egypt', in *RHA* XVIII/66, 57–63.

—— 1961a. 'The god Šuwaliyat reconsidered', in *RHA* XIX/68, 1–18.

—— 1961b. 'Hittite Mythology', in *Mythologies of the Ancient World*, ed. S. N. Kramer. New York.

—— 1962. 'Rituale für die Göttin Ḫuwaššanna', in *Oriens*, 15, 345–51.

—— 1964. 'Religion und Kultus der Hethiter', in *Neuere Hethiterforschung*, ed. G. Walser (*Historia*, Einzelschriften 7).

—— 1965. 'A votive sword with Old Assyrian inscription', in *Studies in Honour of Benno Landsberger on his 75th Birthday, April 21, 1965* (Chicago), 197–8.

—— 1969. 'Some aspects of Hittite festivals', in *Actes de la XVIIe Rencontre Assyriologique Internationale* (Brussels), 175–80.

—— 1971. 'The Hittite palace', in *XIXe Rencontre Assyriologique Internationale* (Paris), 305–14.

—— 1975a. 'The Hittite temple according to written sources', in *Compte rendu de la XXe Rencontre Assyriologique Internationale* (Leiden, 1972), 125–32.

—— 1975b. 'Yazilikaya: apropos a new interpretation', in *JNES* 34, 273–7.

GURNEY, O. R., 1940. 'Hittite Prayers of Mursili II', in *Annals of Archaeology and Anthropology* (Liverpool), 27, 3–163.

—— 1941. Review of Goetze, *The Hittite Ritual of Tunnawi*, in *Journal of the Royal Asiatic Society*, 1941, 56–61.

—— 1958. 'Hittite Kingship', in *Myth, Ritual and Kingship*, ed. S. H. Hooke, 105–21 (Oxford).

HAAS, V., 1970. *Der Kult von Nerik. Ein Beitrag zur hethitischen Kulturgeschichte* (Studia Pohl 4). Rome.

—— 1971. 'Ein hethitisches Beschwörungsmotiv aus Kizzuwatna, seine Herkunft und Bedeutung', in *Orientalia*, 40, 410–30.

—— 1975a. 'Hurri, Šeri und', in *RlA* IV. 506.

—— 1975b. 'Ḫutena, Ḫutellura', in *RlA* IV. 526.

—— and WÄFLER, M., 1974. 'Yazilikaya und der Grosse Tempel', in *Oriens Antiquus*, 13, 211–26.

Haas, V., and Wilhelm, G., 1974. *Hurritische und luwische Riten aus Kizzuwatna* (*Alter Orient und Altes Testament*, Sonderreihe 3). Neukirchen.

Hartmann, H., 1960. *Die Musik der sumerischen Kultur.* Frankfurt-am-Main.

Hoffner, H. A., 1966. 'Symbols for masculinity and femininity', in *JBL* 85, 326–34.

—— 1967a. 'Second millennium antecedents to the Hebrew *'ōbh*', in *JBL* 86, 385–401.

—— 1967b. 'An English–Hittite Glossary', in *RHA* XXV/80, 7–99.

—— 1968a. 'Hittite *tarpiš* and Hebrew *terāphīm*', in *JNES* 27, 61–70.

—— 1968b. 'Birth and name-giving in Hittite texts', in *JNES* 27, 198–203.

—— 1969. 'Some contributions of Hittitology to Old Testament study', in *Tyndale Bulletin*, 20, 27–55.

—— 1973. 'The Hittites and Hurrians', in *Peoples of Old Testament Times*, ed. D. J. Wiseman (Oxford).

—— 1974. *Alimenta Hethaeorum* (American Oriental Series 55). New Haven.

Hogarth, D. G., 1914. *Carchemish*, Part I. (London.) See also Woolley, C. L.

Hooke, S. H., 1938. *The Origins of Early Semitic Ritual* (Schweich Lectures, 1935).

—— 1952. 'The theory and practice of substitution', in *Vetus Testamentum*, 2, 2–17.

Houwink ten Cate, P. H., 1961. *The Luwian Population Groups of Lycia and Cilicia Aspera during the Hellenistic Period.* Leiden.

—— 1967. 'Muwatallis' prayer to the Storm-god of Kummanni', in *RHA* XXV/81, 101–40.

—— 1969. 'Hittite royal prayers', in *Numen*, 16, 81–98.

Hrozný, B., 1932. 'Une inscription de Ras-Šamra en langue churrite', in *Archiv orientální*, 4, 118–29.

Jakob-Rost, L., 1959. Review of Friedrich, *Hethitisches Wörterbuch, 1. Ergänzungsheft*, in *Deutsche Literaturzeitung*, 80, 303–5.

—— 1963. 'Zu den hethitischen Bildbeschreibungen', in *MIO* 8, 161–217, and 9, 175–239.

—— 1972. *Das Ritual der Malli aus Arzawa gegen Behexung* (Texte der Hethiter 2). Heidelberg.

Kaiser, O., 1959. *Die mythische Bedeutung des Meeres in Ägypten, Ugarit und Israel.* Berlin.

Kammenhuber, A., 1955. 'Die protohattisch-hethitische Bilinguis vom Mond der vom Himmel gefallen ist', in *ZA* 51, 102–23.

—— 1959. 'Das Paläische', in *RHA* XVII/64, 1–92.

—— 1962. 'Hattische Studien', in *RHA* XX/70, 1–29.

—— 1964/5. 'Die hethitischen Vorstellungen von Seele und Leib, Herz und Leibesinneren, Kopf und Person', in *ZA* 56, 150–212, and 57, 177–222.

—— 1969. Chapters in *Altkleinasiatische Sprachen* (*Handbuch der Orientalistik* erste Abteilung, zweiter Band, Lieferung 2). Leiden.

—— 1971. 'Heth. *ḫaššuš 2-e ekuzi* "Der König trinkt zwei" ', in *SMEA* 14, 143–59.

—— 1972. Review of *KBo* XVII, in *Orientalia*, 41, 292–302.

—— 1974. 'Historisch-geographische Nachrichten aus der althurrischen Überlieferung, dem altelamischen und den Inschriften der Könige von Akkad für die Zeit vor dem Einfall der Gutäer (ca. 2200/2136)', in *Acta Antiqua Academiae Scientiarum Hungaricae*, 22, 157–247.

—— 1975. 'Ḫesui, Ḫisue', in *RlA* IV. 369–70.

KRAMER, S. N., 1969. *The Sacred Marriage Rite*. Bloomington and London.

KRETSCHMER, P., 1930. 'Der Name der Lykier und andere kleinasiatische Völkernamen', in *Kleinasiatische Forschungen*, I. 1–17.

—— 1950. 'Zwei eigentümliche hethitische Götternamen', in *Archiv orientální*, 17 (1), 413–19.

KRONASSER, H., 1961. 'Fünf hethitische Rituale', in *Die Sprache*, 7, 140–67.

—— 1962. 'Nachträge und Berichtigungen zu 7/1961, 140–67', in *Die Sprache*, 8, 108–13.

KÜHNE, C., and OTTEN, H., 1971. *Der Šaušgamuwa-Vertrag* (*StBoT* 16). Wiesbaden.

KÜMMEL, H. M., 1967. *Ersatzrituale für den hethitischen König* (*StBoT* 3). Wiesbaden.

—— 1968. 'Ersatzkönig und Sündenbock', in *ZAW* 80, 298–318.

—— 1973a. 'Die Religion der Hethiter', in *Theologie und Religionswissenschaft* (Darmstadt), 65–85.

—— 1973b. 'Gesang und Gesanglosigkeit in der hethitischen Kultmusik', in *Festschrift Heinrich Otten*, 169–78.

—— 1975. 'Horn', in *RlA* IV, 469–70.

LAMBERT, W. G., 1957a. 'Ancestors, authors and canonicity', in *JCS* 11, 1–14.

—— 1957b. 'A part of the ritual for the substitute king', in *AfO* 18, 109–12.

—— 1962. 'A catalogue of texts and authors', in *JCS* 16, 59–77.

LAROCHE, E., 1946/7. 'Recherches sur les noms des dieux hittites', in *RHA* VII/46, 7–133 (also separately in book form).

—— 1948a. 'Études "proto-hittites" ', in *Revue d'assyriologie*, 41, 67–98.

—— 1948b. 'Teššub, Hebat et leur cour', in *JCS* 2, 113–36.

—— 1952. 'Le panthéon de Yazilikaya', in *JCS* 6, 115–23.

—— 1954. 'Études sur les hiéroglyphes hittites', in *Syria*, 31, 99–117.

—— 1955a. 'Divinités lunaires d'Anatolie', in *RHR* 148, 1–24.

—— 1955b. 'Études de vocabulaire V', in *RHA* XIII/57, 72–88.

—— 1955c. Review of *IBoT* III, in *RHA* XIII/57, 111–12.

—— 1958a. 'Études de vocabulaire VII', in *RHA* XVI/63, 85–114.

—— 1958b. 'Eflatun Pınar', in *Anatolia*, 3, 43–7.

—— 1959. *Dictionnaire de la langue louvite*. Paris.

—— 1960a. 'Koubaba, déesse anatolienne, et le problème des origines de Cybèle', in *Éléments orientaux dans la religion grecque ancienne*. Paris.

—— 1960b. *Les Hiéroglyphes hittites. Première partie, l'écriture*. Paris.

—— 1961. Review of Otten, *Hethitische Totenrituale*, in *BiOr* 18, 83–4.

—— 1963. 'Le dieu anatolien Sarruma', in *Syria*, 40, 277–302.

LAROCHE, E., 1964/5. 'La prière hittite: vocabulaire et typologie', in *Annuaire, École Pratique des Hautes Études*, 72, 3–29.

—— 1965/8. 'Textes mythologiques hittites en transcription: (1) mythologie anatolienne', in *RHA* XXIII/77, 62–176; (2) 'mythologie d'origine étrangère', ibid. XXVI/82, 7–90. (Also separately, pp. 1–204.)

—— 1966. *Les Noms des Hittites*. Paris.

—— 1967. 'Les noms anatoliens du "dieu" et leurs dérivés', in *JCS* 21, 174–7.

—— 1968. 'Documents en langue hourrite provenant de Ras Shamra', in *Ugaritica*, V, 447–544.

—— 1969. 'Les dieux de Yazilikaya', in *RHA* XXVII/84–5, 61–109.

—— 1970. 'Études de linguistique anatolienne III', in *RHA* XXVIII, 22–78.

—— 1971. *Catalogue des textes hittites*. Paris. (Abbr. *CTH*.)

—— 1972. 'Catalogue des textes hittites, premier supplément', in *RHA* 30, 94–133.

—— 1973. 'Un syncrétisme gréco-anatolien: Sandas-Héraklès', in *Les Syncrétismes dans les religions grecque et romaine* (Paris), 103–14.

—— 1974. 'Les dénominations des dieux "antiques" dans les textes hittites', in *Anatolian Studies presented to Hans Gustav Güterbock on his Sixty-fifth Birthday* (Istanbul), 175–85.

—— 1975. 'La réforme religieuse du roi Tudhaliya IV et sa signification politique', in *Les Syncrétismes dans les religions de l'Antiquité, Colloque de Besançon (22–3 Octobre, 1973)*, ed. F. Dunand et P. Lévêque (Leiden, 1975), 87–95.

LESKY, A., 1927. 'Ein ritueller Scheinkampf bei den Hethitern', in *Archiv für Religionswissenschaft*, 24, 73–82.

LEVY, G. R., 1953. *The Sword from the Rock*. London.

MCCARTHY, D. J., 1963. *Treaty and Covenant*. Rome.

—— 1969. 'The symbolism of blood and sacrifice', in *JBL* 88, 166–76.

MACQUEEN, J. G., 1959. 'Hattian mythology and Hittite monarchy', in *Anatolian Studies*, 9, 171–88.

—— 1975. *The Hittites and their Contemporaries in Asia Minor*. London.

MALAMAT, A., 1955. 'Doctrines of causality in Hittite and Biblical historiography', in *Vetus Testamentum*, 5, 1–12.

MASSON, O., 1950. 'A propos d'un rituel hittite pour la lustration d'une armée: le rite de purification par le passage entre les deux parties d'une victime', in *RHR* 137, 5–25.

MENDENHALL, G., 1954. 'Covenant forms in Israelite tradition', in *The Biblical Archaeologist*, 17, 50–76.

NEU, E., 1968. Review of von Schuler, *Die Kaskäer*, in *Indogermanische Forschungen*, 73, 172.

—— 1970. *Ein althethitisches Gewitterritual* (*StBoT* 12). Wiesbaden.

—— 1974. *Der Anitta-Text* (*StBoT* 18). Wiesbaden.

OETTINGER, N., 1976. *Die militärischen Eide der Hethiter* (*StBoT* 22). Wiesbaden.

ÖZGÜÇ, T., 1957. 'The Bitik vase', in *Anatolia*, 2, 57–78.

—— 1965. 'New finds from Horoztepe', in *Anatolia*, 8, 1–25.

ÖZGÜÇ, T. and N., 1949. *Ausgrabungen in Karahöyük* (Türk Tarih Kurumu Yayinlari V, 7). Ankara.

ORTHMANN, W., 1971. *Untersuchungen zur späthethitischen Kunst.* Bonn.

OTTEN, H., 1942. 'Die Überlieferungen des Telipinu-Mythus', in *MVAG* 46 (1).

—— 1950. 'Die Gottheit Lelvani der Boğazköy-Texte', in *JCS* 4, 119–36.

—— 1952. 'Beiträge zum hethitischen Lexikon', in *ZA* 50, 230–6.

—— 1953a. *Luwische Texte in Umschrift.* Berlin.

—— 1953b. 'Pirva — der Gott auf dem Pferde', in *JKF* 2, 62–73.

—— 1955. Review of *IBoT* III, in *OLZ* 50, 389–94.

—— 1956. 'Ein Text zum Neujahrsfest aus Boğazköy', in *OLZ* 51, 102–5.

—— 1954/6. '^{d}KAL = ^{d}Inar(a)', in *AfO* 17, 369.

—— 1958a. *Hethitische Totenrituale.* Berlin.

—— 1958b. 'Bestattungssitten und Jenseitsvorstellungen nach den hethitischen Texten', *apud* Bittel, 1958 (*WVDOG* 71).

—— 1958c. 'Keilschrifttexte', in *MDOG* 91, 73–84.

—— 1959a. 'Die Götter Nupatik, Pirinkir, Ḫešue und Hatni-Pišaišapḫi in den hethitischen Felsreliefs von Yazilikaya', in *Anatolia,* 4, 27–37.

—— 1959b. 'Ritual bei Erneuerung von Kultsymbolen hethitischer Schutzgottheiten', in *Festschrift Johannes Friedrich,* 351–9.

—— 1961a. 'Das Hethiterreich', in *Kulturgeschichte des Alten Orient,* ed. H. Schmökel (Stuttgart).

—— 1961b. 'Eine Beschwörung der Unterirdischen aus Boğazköy', in *ZA* 54, 114–57.

—— 1962. 'Zu den hethitischen Totenritualen', in *OLZ* 57, 229–33.

—— 1963a. 'Aitiologische Erzählung von der Überquerung des Taurus', in *ZA* 55, 156–68.

—— 1963b. 'Neue Quellen zum Ausklang des Hethitischen Reiches', in *MDOG* 94, 1–23.

—— 1964a. 'Die Religionen des alten Kleinasien', in *Handbuch der Orientalistik,* VIII/1, Lieferung 1.

—— 1964b. 'Der Weg des hethitischen Staates zum Grossreich', in *Saeculum,* 15, 115–24.

—— 1965. 'Der Gott Akni in den hethitischen Texten und seine indoarische Herkunft', in *OLZ* 60, 545–51.

—— 1967. 'Zur Datierung und Bedeutung des Felsheiligtums von Yazilikaya', in *ZA* 58, 222–40.

—— 1971. *Ein hethitisches Festritual* (*StBoT* 13). Wiesbaden.

—— 1973a. *Eine althethitische Erzählung um die Stadt Zalpa* (*StBoT* 17). Wiesbaden.

—— 1973b. 'Das Ritual der Allī aus Arzawa', in *ZA* 63, 76–82.

—— 1974. 'Die Schenkungsurkunde KUB XIII 8—eine junge Kopie', in *Anatolian Studies presented to Hans Gustav Güterbock on his Sixty-fifth Birthday* (Istanbul), 245–51.

—— 1975. Articles in *RlA* IV.

OTTEN, H., and SIEGELOVA, J., 1970. 'Die hethitischen Gulš-Gottheiten und die Erschaffung der Menschen', in *AfO* 23, 32–8.

—— and VON SODEN, W., 1968. *Das akkadisch-hethitische Vokabular KBo. I 44 + KBo. XIII 1* (*StBoT* 7). Wiesbaden.

—— and SOUČEK, V., 1969. *Ein althethitisches Ritual für das Königspaar* (*StBoT* 8). Wiesbaden.

PAGE, D., 1973. *Folktales in Homer's Odyssey*. Harvard University Press.

PRITCHARD, J. P. (ed.), 1969. *Ancient Near Eastern Texts relating to the Old Testament*, 3rd edn. Princeton. (Abbr. *ANET*.)

REED, W. L., 1949. *The Asherah in the Old Testament*.

—— 1962. 'Asherah', in *Interpreter's Dictionary of the Bible*, A–D, 250–2.

REINER, E., and GÜTERBOCK, H. G., 1967. 'The great prayer to Ishtar and its two versions from Boğazköy', in *JCS* 21, 255–66.

RIEMSCHNEIDER, M., 1954. *Die Welt der Hethiter*. Stuttgart.

RITTER, E. K., 1965. 'Magical-expert (= *Āšipu*) and physician (=*Asû*): notes on two complementary professions in Babylonian medicine', in *Studies in Honour of Benno Landsberger on his Seventy-fifth Birthday* (Assyriological Studies 16). Chicago.

RÖLLIG, W., 1975. 'Hazzi', in *RlA* IV, 241–2.

ROST, LEONHARD, 1958. 'Erwägungen zum israelitischen Brandopfer', in *Von Ugarit nach Kumran, Eissfeldt Festschrift* (*ZAW*, Beiheft 77), 177–83.

ROST, LIANE, 1953. 'Ein hethitisches Ritual gegen Familienzwist', in *MIO* 1, 345–79. (See also JAKOB-ROST.)

SAYCE, A. H., 1919. 'The scapegoat among the Hittites', in *Expository Times*, 31, 283–4.

SCHULER, E. VON, 1965a. *Die Kaskäer*. Berlin.

—— 1965b. 'Kleinasien: die Mythologie der Hethiter und Hurriter', in *Wörterbuch der Mythologie*, I. 141–215.

—— 1969. '*marnu'ātum* — ein kleinasiatisches Lehnwort im Altassyrischen', in *lišan mitḫurti, Festschrift Wolfram Freiherr von Soden* (*Alter Orient und Altes Testament* 1, Neukirchen), 317–22.

SCHWARTZ, B., 1938. 'The Hittite and Luwian ritual of Zarpiya of Kezzuwatna', in *JAOS* 58, 334–53.

—— 1947. 'A Hittite ritual text', in *Orientalia*, 16, 23–55.

SIEGELOVA, J., 1971. *Appu-Märchen und Ḫedammu-Mythus* (*StBoT* 14). Wiesbaden.

SMITH, W. ROBERTSON, 1901. *The Religion of the Semites* (new edn.). London.

SOMMER, F., and EHELOLF, H., 1924. *Das hethitische Ritual des Pāpanikri von Komana* (*KBo. V 1 = Bo. 2001*) (Boghazköi-Studien 10). Leipzig.

STAUDER, W., 1961. *Die Harfen und Leiern Vorderasiens in babylonischer und assyrischer Zeit*. Frankfurt-am-Main.

—— 1970. 'Die Musik der Sumerer, Babylonier und Assyrer', in *Handbuch der Orientalistik*, 1. Abt., Ergänzungsband, 4, 171–254.

—— 1975. 'Harfe', in *RlA* IV, 114–20; 'Horn', ibid. 470–1.

STEINER, G., 1966. 'Gott: (D) Nach hethitischen Texten', in *RlA* III, 547–75.

STEINER, G., 1971. 'Die Unterweltsbeschwörung des Odysseus im Lichte hethitischer Texte', in *Ugarit-Forschungen*, 3, 265–83.

SZABÓ, G., 1971. *Ein hethitisches Entsühnungsritual für das Königspaar Tuthaliya und Nikalmati* (Texte der Hethiter 1). Heidelberg.

VAUGHAN, P. H., 1974. *The Meaning of 'bāmâ' in the Old Testament*. Cambridge.

VAUX, R. DE, 1964. *Studies in Old Testament Sacrifice*. Cardiff.

VIEYRA, M., 1939. 'Rites de purification hittites', in *RHR* 119, 121–53.

—— 1955. *Hittite Art*. London.

—— 1957. 'Ištar de Nineveh', in *Revue d'assyriologie*, 51, 83–102.

—— 1961. 'Les noms du "mundus" en hittite et en assyrien et la pythonesse d'Endor', in *RHA* XIX/69, 47–55.

—— 1965. 'Ciel et enfer hittites', in *Revue d'assyriologie*, 59, 127–30.

WEIDNER, E., 1923. *Politische Dokumente aus Kleinasien*. (Boghazköi-Studien 8–9). Leipzig.

WEIHER, E. VON, 1975. Articles in *RlA* IV.

WOOLLEY, (C.) L., 1921. *Carchemish*, Part II. London.

—— 1952. *Carchemish*, Part III. London.

ZACCAGNINI, C., 1974. 'Šattiwaz(z)a', in *Oriens Antiquus*, 13, 25–34.

INDEX

I. GENERAL

II. NAMES OF DEITIES

III. HITTITE WORDS AND SUMEROGRAMS

a. Yazilikaya, Chamber A. The central group

b. Yazilikaya, Chamber A. The line of gods

Yazilikaya, relief in Chamber B. Tudhaliya IV in the protective embrace of his god Sarruma

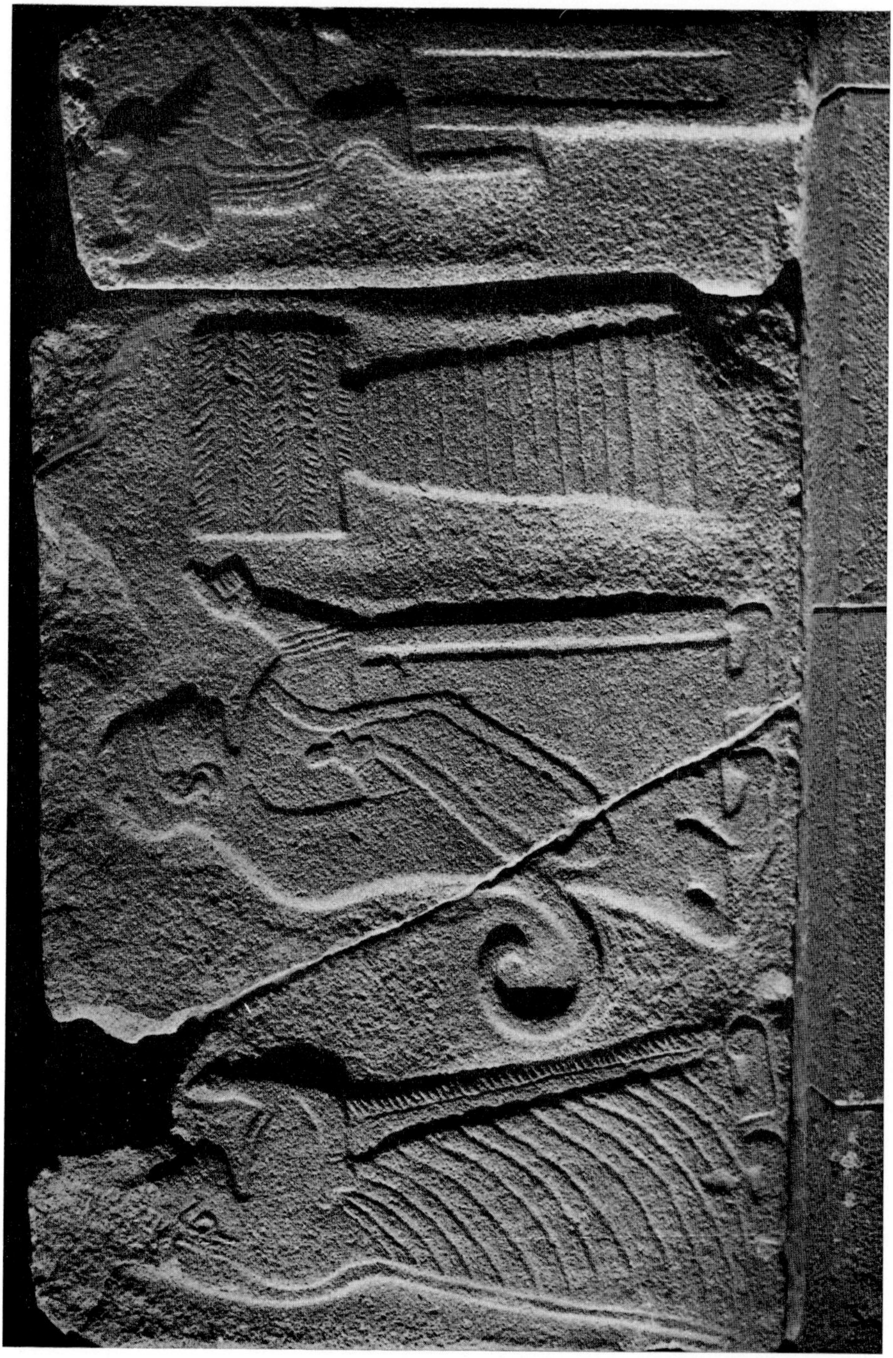

Relief from Alaca Hüyük. The king worshipping Teshub in the form of a bull

PLATE IV

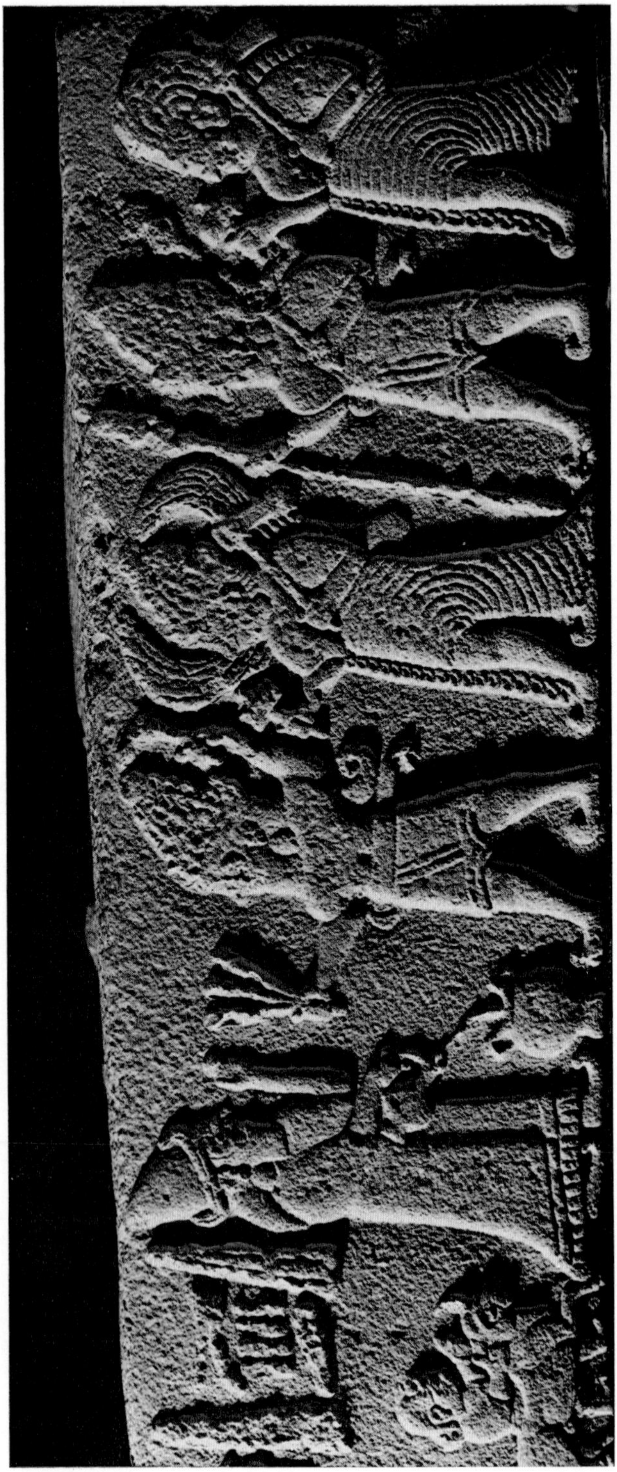

Late Hittite relief from Malatya. The king pouring a libation before the Weather-god, Ishtar, and two other deities

PLATE V

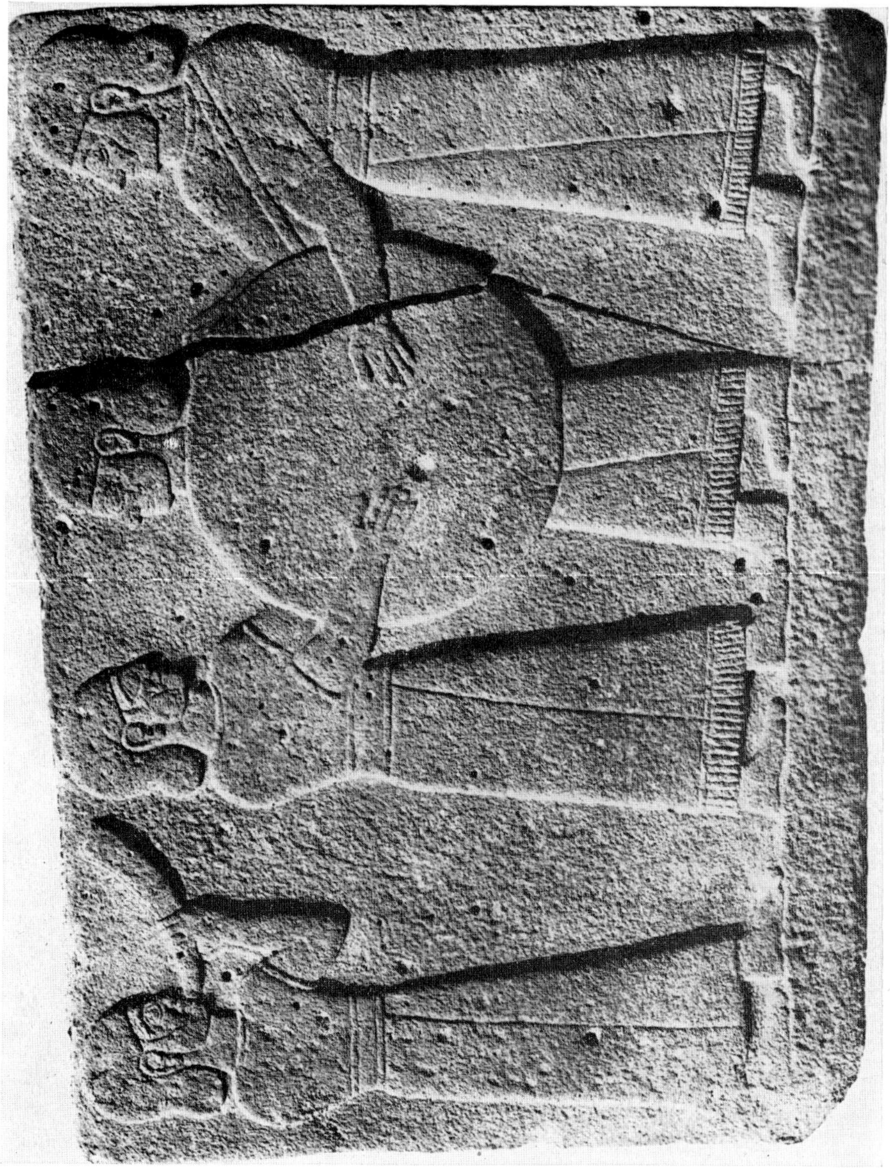

Relief from Carchemish showing musicians playing a horn and a large drum or gong

PLATE VI

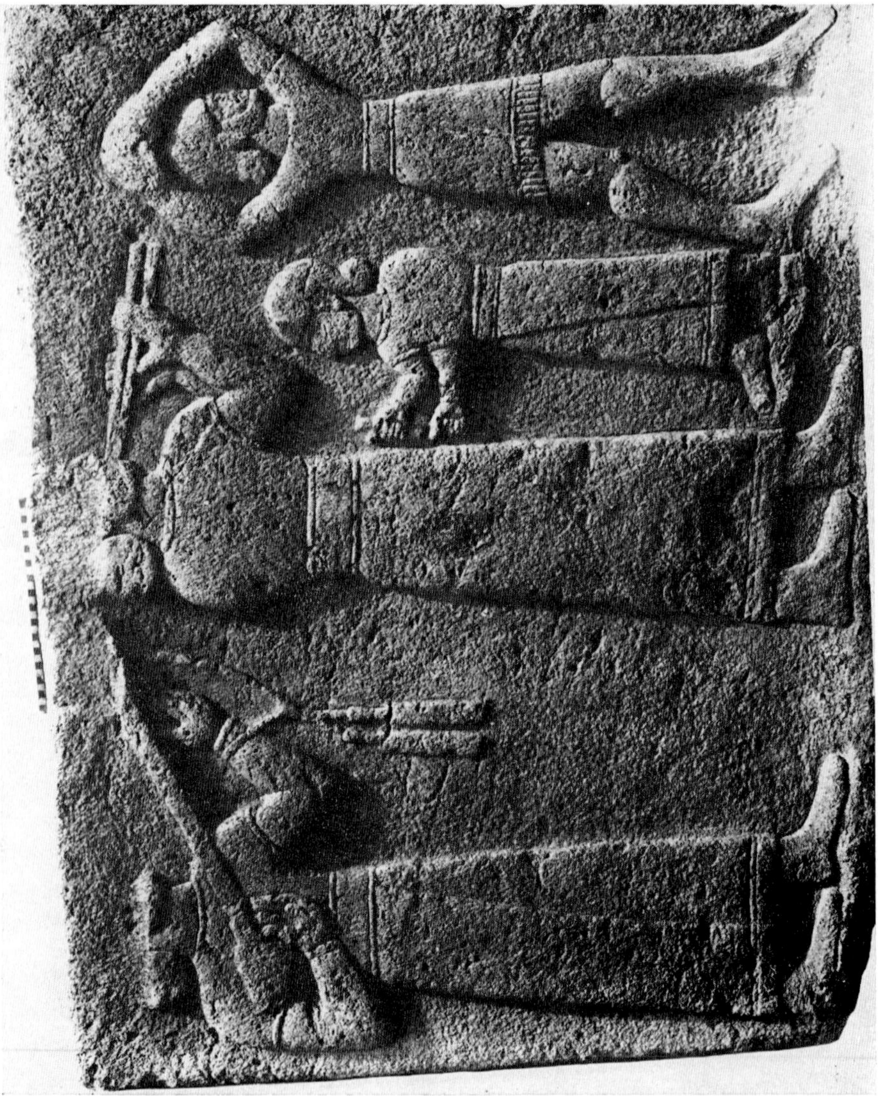

Relief from Carchemish showing musicians playing a lute and double pipes

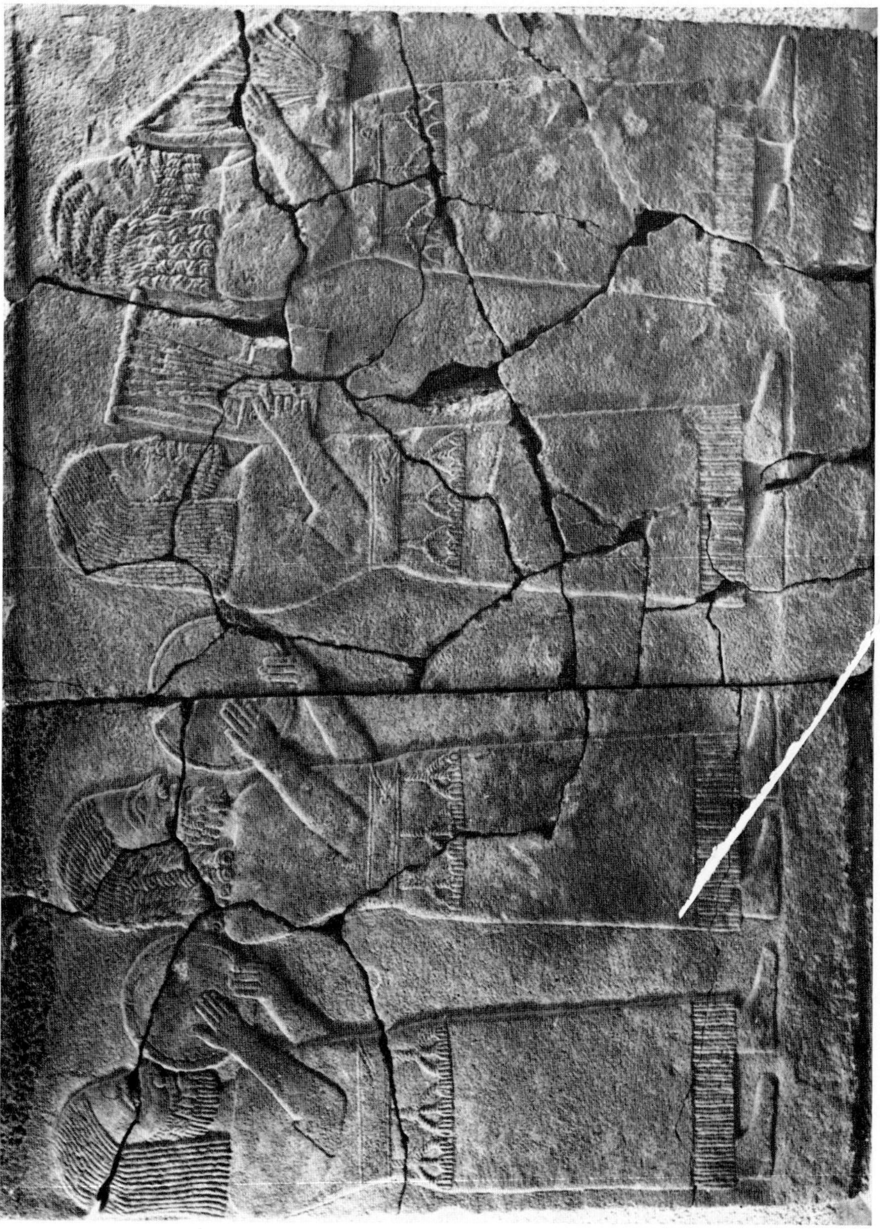

Relief from Zincirli showing musicians playing two kinds of lyre and tambourines

PLATE VIII

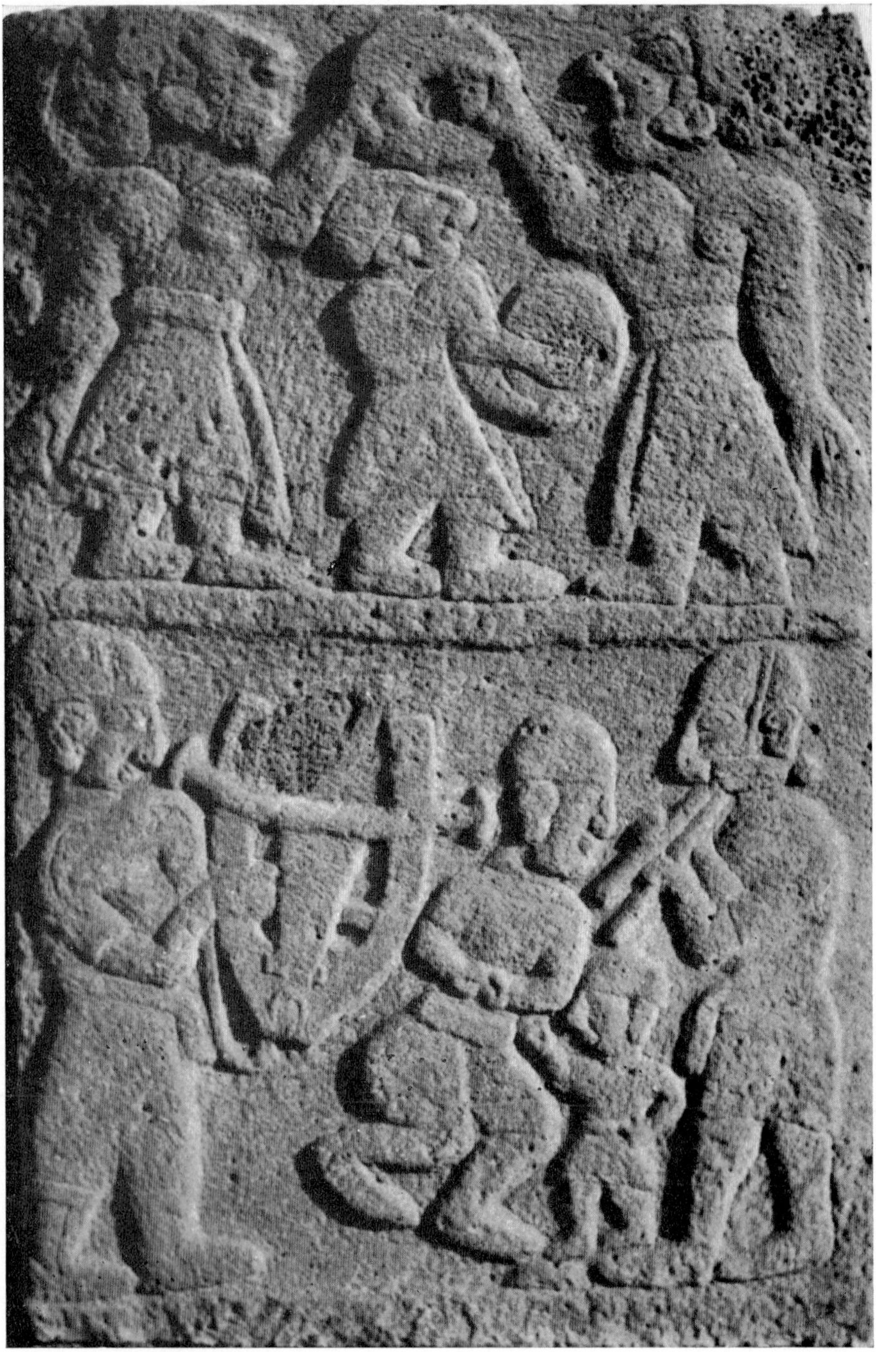

Relief from Karatepe showing musicians playing a lyre, double pipes, and tambourines(?)